MONTANA'S BITTERROOT VALLEY
Just Short of Paradise

BY RUSS LAWRENCE

The best of the Bitterroot to you!

Russ Lawrence

MONTANA'S BITTERROOT VALLEY
Just Short of Paradise

BY RUSS LAWRENCE

Photography by Harry June

Copyright 1999 by Russell Lawrence

Library of Congress Catalog Card No. 99-75625

ISBN 0-912299-88-6 (Hardcover)
ISBN 0-912299-89-4 (Softcover)

STONEYDALE PRESS PUBLISHING COMPANY
523 Main Street • P.O. Box 188
Stevensville, Montana 59870
Phone: 406-777-2729

TABLE OF CONTENTS

Acknowledgments

I wish to thank all those who helped me with the research for this book, including the people who contributed to my knowledge of the valley even before I knew I was writing a book. The following is a short list that should be much longer; I suspect many names are missing from this list, and I regret any omissions.

Helen Bibler; Linda Bieber; Bitterroot National Forest (USDA Forest Service); Bitterroot Valley Chamber of Commerce; Bitter Root Valley Historical Society; Dixie Dies; Jim Freeman; Henry Grant; Mary Horstman; Ray Hunter; Martha Jessop; Doug Johnson (Daly Mansion Preservation Trust); Jack Losenski; Montana Dept. of Fish, Wildlife and Parks; Erma Owings; Ada Powell; Ravalli County Museum; Jim Story; John Ormiston.

Dedication

This book is dedicated to those whose loss was greatest, the Bitterroot Salish.

MONTANA'S BITTERROOT VALLEY:
Just Short of Paradise

PREFACE

The Bitterroot Valley is defined geographically by the mountains that cradle it, and by the river at its heart. To attempt to define the Bitterroot in any terms beyond the strictly physical is a hopeless task; to describe it, on the other hand, is the goal of this book.

Words and pictures can only go so far, though. The sounds of songbirds calling (or the rowdy cackling of magpies), the rush of tumbling clear waters, and the soft whump of fresh snow falling from pine boughs to the ground below can't be contained within these pages. So, too, the scents of delicate wildflowers or fresh-mown hay are yours to discover on your own.

This book is only intended as an introduction to the history, natural history, resources and culture of the Bitterroot Valley. Where other books provide greater depth, this one will summarize. But books aren't the best way to acquaint oneself with the area. Truly getting to know the Bitterroot means getting involved with the people who live here, visiting the vastness of the Selway-Bitterroot Wilderness, spending some quality time on the river, and just enjoying the passage of the seasons in a place where scenic splendor is a given.

The Bitterroot Valley has never been a paradise – though many have thought it came close. The Salish lived happily for centuries in this place, hunting deer and elk, and gathering roots, herbs and berries. The valley was remote enough to discourage raids by the more war-like plains tribes, but because their lives depended on the buffalo, these peaceful people still had to make the perilous trip across the mountains to hunt.

Lewis & Clark found a beautiful valley, inhabited by a hospitable people who willingly traded them the horses they needed to make a success of their voyage to the Pacific. They also endured the greatest hardships of the expedition, getting to and from the Bitterroot near Lost Trail and Lolo Passes.

Early settlers found that the valley's climate was largely suitable for growing produce to feed Montana's boisterous early mining camps, but it's still the northern

...lassic U-shaped valley of Blodgett Canyon, with its steep-faced walls, ...cteristic of glacial action. Most of the valleys in the Bitterroot's east face ...t this, while the somewhat lower Sapphire Range largely escaped it. (R. ...ence photo)

Rockies: tinder-dry in summer, prone to killing frosts that can shorten the growing season from either end, and subject to brief but intense outbreaks of arctic cold in winter.

Those who made a living from the valley's natural resources in the 20th century found those resources to be generous but not boundless, and that their exploitation had consequences they hadn't anticipated. The Bitterroot's distance from major markets and sometimes-problematic access to transportation stymied more than one attempt to develop its natural riches, although others flourished.

The valley's history is rife with the stories of people who moved here believing they had found the perfect place, only to find that the many small but inescapable irritations of climate, geography and culture were more than they wanted to deal with. Residents have earned a reputation for being ornery and contentious when it comes to issues, although quick to help a neighbor in need.

Those who live here now find that the Bitterroot is paradise with a slow leak, difficult to plug. The valley's best attributes – its rural nature, breathtaking scenery, pristine river, small-town character – are slowly diminishing, while the worst of the rest of the world occasionally leaks in. Hints of urban social problems crop up now and then, while traffic builds up on once-lonely roads now increasingly lined by strip development.

And yet, by any rational measure, it remains a highly desirable place to live.

Here, then, is a portrait of a place that offers a challenge with every opportunity, and a reward for every hardship. That's the Bitterroot experience we all have in common.

ORIENTATION

The Bitterroot Valley stretches for roughly 100 miles south of Missoula. It is bounded on the west by the Bitterroot Mountains, on the east by the Sapphire Range, and on the south by the Continental Divide at the Idaho border, the river's headwaters.

The valley floor is roughly ten miles wide for much of its lower reaches. Largely flat, in springtime and summer the agricultural land is graced by apple blossoms and extensive fields of alfalfa and grass hay. The river wanders, unhurried, through braided channels, creating extensive wetland habitat – and providing much-needed irrigation water in an arid valley.

Most of the valley's 35,000 or so inhabitants live in this broad, lower reach, where good soils and a reasonably mild climate prevail.

Between Hamilton and Darby the mountains begin to encroach, and in its upper reaches above Darby the Bitterroot is characterized by narrowing mountain canyons that still open surprisingly in places. The river gradient steepens, too, above Darby, and with higher elevation comes a harsher climate and generally poorer soils. Both the East Fork and the West Fork drainages of the Bitterroot River occasionally broaden into lush pasture and hayfields, but both close in again as you arrive at their headwaters.

Geographically, the valley's northern limit would be just north of Lolo, where the foothills pinch down to the river as it enters the Missoula valley. The remaining boundaries naturally encompass the Bitterroot River drainage – along the crest of the

Bitterroot mountain range on the west and south, and the top of the Sapphire range to the east.

U.S. Highway 93 traverses the valley from Missoula in the north on its way south to the Idaho border, providing year-round access to the Bitterroot. The only all-weather road that leads out of the valley to the west is U.S. 12, which follows meandering Lolo Creek west from Lolo, shadowing the tracks of Lewis and Clark over Lolo pass to the Lochsa river and Idaho's Clearwater country. The Skalkaho Highway winds east from Hamilton over Skalkaho Pass to Philipsburg and the upper Rock Creek area, but is unpaved over the pass, and closed in winter.

The East Fork Road provides access to that valley and the Anaconda-Pintler Wilderness, and over the crest into the Big Hole Valley. Montana Highway 43 joins U.S. 93 at Lost Trail Pass, providing a paved link to the scenic Big Hole Valley.

The West Fork Road offers two seasonal routes out of the valley, for those with suitable vehicles. Following it past Painted Rocks Reservoir, Forest Service roads can take you over the mountains to the Salmon river in Idaho, a beautiful trip when the roads are clear of snow. Or, you can follow it 101 miles over Nez Perce Pass, to the Selway river, and on to Elk City in Idaho. This narrow, unimproved road defines a narrow corridor that is boxed in between the 1.3-million acre Selway-Bitterroot Wilderness to the north, and the 2.3-million acre Frank Church-River of No Return Wilderness to the south. This is a trip that will take you deep in to the heart of America's premier wilderness backcounty.

PART ONE: NATURAL HISTORY

GEOLOGY

The Bitterroot Valley is dominated by its two mountain ranges, the Bitterroot mountains to the west and the Sapphire range on the east. Many of the peaks in the Bitterroot range rise to over 9,000 feet above sea level, and the highest, Trapper Peak, soars to 10,157. The somewhat gentler Sapphires typically top out about a thousand feet lower.

Running almost due north and south, the Bitterroot mountains are riven by canyon after canyon, in the bottom of each a tumbling mountain stream running due east to the river. The Sapphire range, in contrast, is drained by a series of streams with a more dendritic pattern – that is, like the veins in a leaf, splitting into ever smaller streams that finger their way into the mountains.

The two ranges, separated by only a few miles, have less in common than you might think, geologically speaking. The northern end of the Bitterroots feature a mix of sedimentary mudstones (argillite), metamorphic gneiss and intrusive granite, but south of St. Mary's Peak (which the Salish called "Red Mountain") the composition changes almost exclusively to the granite of the Idaho Batholith, formed deep below the earth's surface. The Sapphires, in contrast, are a mongrel range, featuring a mix of granite foothills, supporting layers of sedimentary rocks deposited at the bottom of an ancient sea, predominantly argillite, with igneous outcroppings here and there. From an area north of Darby on to the southern reaches of the valley, igneous rhyolite becomes more common.

According to the most current theories, the Bitterroot Range was formed perhaps 70 million years ago when a large bubble of molten granite magma began to rise from deep within the earth, forcing its way up through the overlying rock. Here's where it gets jaw-droppingly farfetched: geologists with straight faces now suggest that the rising body of molten magma "greased the skids," so to speak, and that the existing rocks above it more or less just slid off that big bubble of rising magma. Part of the slab that "slid off" now forms the Sapphire mountain range, and the Bitterroots, part of that igneous bubble, now stand in what was once their place.

If this theory is too much for you, there are plenty of people willing to believe something more conventional – but nobody's come up with it yet. Stand in the mouth of Blodgett Canyon to observe the evidence that supports this theory: the "slabby" rock formations that form the east face of the Bitterroot range are mylonite, a form of metamorphosed granite or gneiss, that even looks a bit like the frosting that's left behind when the top layer of a cake slides off.

hly-efficient predator of squirrels and other small game, the pine marten (a
er of the weasel family) is a rarely seen resident of the valley's heavily-forested
ountry.

So the top layer of the cake was ten miles thick and slid 50 miles east. It was a big cake.

In this grossly simplified view of the process, the Bitterroot valley is just the trough between the migrating Sapphire slab and the intrusive granite.

About 2.5 million years ago the climate cooled, and the first of several "ice ages" began, spawning energetic glaciers that carved the characteristic "**U**"-shaped canyons of the valley's west side. The last of these probably melted only 10,000 years ago – the blink of an eye, geologically speaking leaving behind huge piles of rocks they had bulldozed out of the mountains; these moraines are still visible at the mouths of the canyons, extending further onto the valley floor the further south you look. High up in the heads of these canyons are typical glacial "cirques," basins where you now find beautiful alpine lakes.

More recently, the valley was part of a huge fresh-water lake, the incredible origins of which nearly rival the mountain-building theory above. Imagine:

About 15,000 years ago, near the end of the last Ice Age, a huge glacier creeping south out of Canada into Idaho backed up the Clark Fork river, flooding the entire watershed. When the water level became deep enough, nearly 2,000 feet at the dam, it floated or breached the glacier, causing the huge lake to drain catastrophically

The Como Peaks loom over the Bitterroot River between Hamilton and Darby. The deep mantle of snow they accumulate all winter melts away to feed the river through the spring and summer.

and producing the world's largest floods, which swept across eastern Washington, creating the "scablands" there.

This flooding occurred dozens of times, over a thousand years or so. "Glacial Lake Missoula," as it's called, filled, emptied, and re-filled more than 40 times as the glacier advanced and was in turn breached. The many shorelines of this ancient lake are most visible on Mount Sentinel and Mount Jumbo in Missoula. The highest lake levels would have filled the Bitterroot valley up to an elevation of about 4,300 feet, roughly lapping at the doorstep of the Conner store.

The glaciation of the Bitterroot mountains and the filling-and-emptying of this awesome lake did have some beneficial side effects, though. For one, the valley is filled with glacial debris, providing rock gardeners with plenty of raw materials. More importantly, it left deposits of fine soil in many areas from Hamilton to Florence, where you now find the hayfields that support the Bitterroot's agricultural base.

CLIMATE

The climate of the Bitterroot varies considerably with elevation, as well as from west to east, but in the valley where most people reside it is remarkably mild...for the northern Rockies.

The tranquility of the Lee Metcalf National Wildlife Refuge just north of Stevensville is appreciated not only by the animals protected therein, but by thousands of people seeking refuge from the bustling development of the Bitterroot. (Billie Linkletter photo)

The dominant factor is moisture – or more precisely, the lack of it. The valley floor is very nearly a desert, averaging only 12-15 inches of rain a year in Hamilton. Trees grow mostly along river and stream courses, and by August only natural wetlands and irrigated fields are still green.

While moist, Pacific air dominates the weather patterns, the Bitterroot Mountains modify it by wringing much of that moisture out, leaving the valley in what is known as their "rain shadow." Where the crest of the Bitterroot range may receive over a hundred inches of moisture annually, the valley gets little more than a tenth of that. Then, as moist air encounters the Sapphire range, it once again begins to yield some of that moisture, becoming nearly as wet as the Bitterroots at their crest.

Winters are relatively mild, by northern Rockies standards. The Continental Divide effectively keeps many of the winter's arctic fronts from affecting the valley's weather, although the occasional icy blast still pours over that rampart. Winter temperatures may go as low as -39F, and the valley on average experiences a dozen days of sub-zero cold, which can occur any time from October through March.

John Owen, one of the valley's most prominent early settlers, starkly illustrated the valley's erratic winter weather with two journal entries, noting on Jan. 3, 1868, that according to an old saying, "the three first days in January govern the remainder

The winter sun sets as a snowstorm clears near Chief Joseph Pass. (R. Lawrence photo)

of the winter – well, if so, we will have a mild, open winter, for the past three days have been quite soft and mild."

A week later he had changed his tune: "Jan. 10: So cold in fact that grown chickens tumble over frozen stiff in daytime." So much for old sayings.

Snow accumulations also vary by elevation, the valley floor receiving only a fraction of what the high country accumulates. At the crest of the mountains, this can be four to ten feet in the Bitterroots, and two to six feet in the Sapphires. The total annual snowfall at Hamilton averages about 40", with rarely more than a few inches on the ground at any given time.

The mountain snowpack usually begins accumulating in October, peaks in April, and is largely gone by July, although a few permanent snowfields persist year-round.

Summer temperatures are relatively mild, Hamilton averaging 85 degrees Fahrenheit in July, occasionally topping 100 degrees Fahrenheit, but always cooling off pleasurably in the evening (the average July low is 51 degrees Fahrenheit). The higher one goes, the cooler it will be, and in the high country wintry conditions may arise in any month.

Gardeners and orchardists take note: July is the only month in which the National Weather Service has not recorded a frost in Hamilton – but that doesn't mean it can't happen. The growing season varies dramatically from one place to another in the valley, some drainages being prone to frosts, some benches seeming regularly to escape them. Generally, the period between Memorial Day and Labor Day brackets the frost-free season – but don't gamble on it.

TABLE: HAMILTON WEATHER

	Jan	Feb	Mar	Apr	May	June	July	Aug	Sept	Oct	Nov	Dec
Abs. max	62	71	74	90	102	100	103	102	98	90	72	66
Avg. max	34	39	49	60	68	75	85	83	72	60	46	37
Avg. min.	16	19	26	33	40	46	51	49	42	34	25	19
Abs. min.	-36	-39	-14	1	18	29	33	32	18	-1	-24	-30
Precip.	.86	.79	.71	.81	1.56	1.76	.77	.70	1.05	.96	.96	.84

FLORA

From an aerial perspective, the dominant biological feature of the Bitterroot is the contrast between forested and open ground. The character of the forest varies wildly between the valley bottom and the mountain tops, but anywhere sufficient moisture falls to support them, you will find trees.

The most familiar tree (and the state tree of Montana) is the Ponderosa pine,

which grows abundantly in the lower elevations. This graceful giant was the dominant species when humans first arrived in the valley. An important lumber species still, it can live for centuries and grow over a hundred feet tall. Easily identified by its long needles and large, prickly cones, its black bark gradually turns to a cinnamon-red as it ages, and the oldest specimens sport a yellowish tinge. It is also known variously as yellow pine and bull pine.

Get up close to a mature Ponderosa pine and smell the bark – it gives off a pleasant, vanilla-scented odor. Indians at one time used to strip the bark from these trees and eat the nutritious cambium (or inner bark) layer, when no other food sources were available. You can see examples of this at the Indian Trees campground in the south end of the valley.

Above the valley floor, on moister sites, the Ponderosa pine gives way to the Douglas-fir. Short needles and a distinctive cone mark this other important timber species.

Fire has played an interesting part in the relationship between these two trees where their habitats overlap. Until man started controlling fires a hundred years ago, wildfires swept the Rockies on a regular basis, averaging perhaps every twenty-five years or so in this area. A Ponderosa pine seedling quickly develops a thick, platy bark that can survive a moderately intense fire. Douglas-fir saplings, in contrast, are much more susceptible to fire. This difference in fire-resistance led to open, park-like stands of pine predominating on the lower elevations of the forest.

Since the era of fire control, though, there has been little to keep the Douglas-fir from encroaching. Being more tolerant of shade, it can spring up under the pine canopy and crowd out the pine seedlings. The balance of the forest has consequently tipped heavily to favor the Douglas-fir, which you now find in thick stands where it could never establish itself before.

Higher still, you will encounter extensive stands of lodgepole pine. This species has actually adapted to the recurrence of fire, and reproduces best after a burn. It is joined in moister, higher-elevation sites by Engelmann spruce and subalpine fir.

At middle elevations stretching as far south as Mill creek, you can find the western larch. This is the very southern edge of their range, but they are beautiful trees, similar in habit to the Douglas-fir. At the highest elevations you can find their close relative, the subalpine larch. This species is rare, and the Bitterroot is one of the few places where it grows. Larches are unique, being the only deciduous conifer – that is, they lose their needles in the autumn. Come late September the larch turn gold, announcing their presence with splashes and slashes of color across the mountainsides and at their peaks.

Other major species you may find on the mountains and in the canyons include western red cedar, grand fir, limber pine, and whitebark pine.

Along the rivers and lining many roads you will find the fast-growing cottonwood, which has the annoying habit of shedding limbs in high winds – beware. Somewhat higher up grows its relative, the quaking aspen. Aspen leaves grow on a flattened petiole, or stem, which causes them to flutter in the slightest breeze. It is a

rosa pine, Montana's state tree, dominates the drier, low-elevation sites in the
root.

picturesque sight, even more so in the fall when the leaves turn golden. Aspen frequently are among the first trees to colonize a site after a fire or other disturbance, such as an avalanche.

Lower your eyes from the forest canopy, and you will find an abundance of wildflowers. As soon as the snow retreats, the Bitterroot offers a tremendous variety of wildflowers, and as the year progresses it seems it's always Spring at some elevation. At the highest elevations, you can still find flowers blooming in August, even though their growing season may only be measured in weeks.

Glacier lilies, wild orchids, arnica, arrowleaf balsamroot, beargrass, and Indian paintbrush are found in many places throughout the West, but the lovely bitterroot flower and the hated knapweed are the signature species of this valley.

Lewisia Rediviva

Meriwether Lewis collected a specimen of the bitterroot and took it back East where, after a period of years in storage, it revived and bloomed. Botanists honored both Lewis and the tenacious little plant by giving it the scientific name of <u>*Lewisia rediviva*</u>*.*

The bitterroot, the Montana state flower, is a small plant with a showy blossom, ranging in color from white to pink to pale lavender, that appears on dry

A high meadow comes alive with beargrass blossoms in July.

hillsides between late May and late June. The plant that produces this somewhat rare flower is a small, nondescript stalk with a root that was an important food source for the native peoples of this area. They would dig the bitterroot in the Spring, then pound and dry the root before preparing it in a number of ways.

Spotted knapweed is, in many ways, the bitterroot's evil twin. The bitterroot is a native plant, knapweed is introduced. Like the bitterroot, knapweed prefers dry sites, but while the bitterroot is fairly fussy about its habitat, spotted knapweed has taken over large areas of the valley, thriving on rocky, parched soils. It is mildly allelopathic, meaning it gives off chemicals that inhibit the growth of other plants. The bitterroot is edible (if not particularly palatable), whereas most animals can't (or won't) eat knapweed, although sheep and goats find it attractive in the spring. The bitterroot is fragile; knapweed is the herbal equivalent of Godzilla. Late in the summer, knapweed's distinctive purple blossom advertises its one useful attribute: bees can make delicious honey from its flowers.

Savvy summertime hikers can feast and doctor themselves with an enticing variety of wild edible and medicinal plants. The edibles range from delectable morel and shaggymane mushrooms to wild asparagus, and include huckleberries, wild strawberries, raspberries, gooseberries, elderberries, chokecherries and Oregon grape...and those are just the ones you can make jam or jelly from. Pick up a reliable

The Bitterroot Valley's lovely namesake, the bitterroot (Lewisia rediviva). (Photo Barbara June)

field guide for a good many more.

Medicinal wild plants are also abundant in the Bitterroot. Consult a field guide, or watch for "herb walks" conducted periodically by local experts.

FAUNA

If you're a large game animal native to the Northern Rockies, then you probably call the Bitterroot home. These animals – including whitetail and mule deer, elk, moose, mountain goats, bighorn sheep and black bear – are the usual winners in popularity contests, but they are by no means the only animal attractions here. Nobody knows exactly how many species of birds, bugs, reptiles and amphibians share the valley with us, but it remains remarkably easy to see a fair sampling of them all.

This rich variety of wildlife is due to the extremely varied habitats the area offers. The river bottom and nearby wetlands offer very moist, sometimes marshy homes to creatures that dwell in water or mud. The upland benches on both sides of the valley provide a drier home with mixed forest and grassland habitats; the canyons support a cool, moist environment on their north-facing sides, while a much drier and

Indian paintbrush enlivens many mountainsides in the Bitterroot. The flower itself is a rather humdrum affair, but the surrounding bracts and upper leaves develop intense red hues. The roots of the paintbrush have evolved the fascinating habit of piercing the roots of nearby plants to steal their food supply.

warmer picture emerges on the south-facing sides. The forests that blanket the flanks of the mountains on both sides of the valley offer still another range of habitats, and a unique set of wildlife that uses each. Finally, the Bitterroot river itself is home to fish, insects, and to water-loving mammals such as beaver, muskrat, mink, and river otter.

Between the river and the higher benches live a rich variety of wildlife, but mostly what you'll see are whitetail deer skirting lawns and pastures. These transitional areas offer the finest habitat for most species, our own included. This is where cities, towns, and rural subdivisions complicate the lives of the local fauna.

While some pastures and hayfields manage to provide cover for nesting birds, in most cultivated areas wildlife are interlopers and not welcome. Badgers, marmots and ground squirrels dig troublesome holes, deer and elk eat crops intended for livestock, and black bears are a nuisance whether they're in the garbage or the beehives or the orchard.

Agricultural land does, however, provide habitat for pheasant and chukars, rabbits and mice, and their predators such as red fox and coyotes. Here also is prime real estate for skunks.

The lower reaches of the mountain canyons offer still more wildlife viewing opportunities. Here, at various times of the year, you may find mule deer and

Pond lilies grace some of the ponds and sloughs in the valley. Their seeds and, to some extent their roots, are edible. (Photo Barbara June)

*Larkspur may be abundant, but that's a mixed blessing: it conte
alkaloids poisonous to cattle, though not to sheep.*

*The glacier lily (also commonly known as the dogtooth viol
one of the first flowers to bloom as the snow recedes. A wel
sight in the spring, its leaves are also edible, with a plea
peppery taste. Go easy on them, though, and leave some fo
bears. (Photo Barbara June)*

*The Fourth of July on a high mountain trail, and suddenly a
redolent scent nearly overcomes you. Must be beargrass, wit
showy, aromatic flower that can't be mistaken. Curse the slip
saw-edged clumps of leaves that can make a steep hil
treacherous in any other season, but in early summer the sc
heavenly, if it doesn't completely overcome you.*

whitetail deer, elk, moose, mountain lion, black bear, and you may have the opportunity to see bighorn sheep and mountain goats. Beavers, raccoon, mink, weasels and even bobcats may happen by, and if you bring a picnic plan to share it with a chipmunk or a ground squirrel. Look up to find the pine squirrel scolding you, and in winter look around in the trees and brush for the tracks of snowshoe hares, whose coats change colors with the seasons.

Lee Metcalf National Wildlife Refuge – Teller Refuge

The 2,800-acre Lee Metcalf National Wildlife Refuge just north of Stevensville is an excellent place to view much of our native wildlife. The varied lowland habitats include ponds, grasslands, pine groves, streams, and cultivated fields. The system of ponds adjacent to the river attracts a huge variety of bird life: ducks, Canadian and snow geese, tundra swans, osprey, bald eagles, great blue herons, hawks, owls and more, depending on the migratory season. Also abundant are whitetail deer, coyotes, pheasant, and Columbian ground squirrels, and lucky visitors may also see foxes. Less lucky visitors may encounter skunks.

The Refuge offers brochures on birds, wildflowers, and other species that may be found there. The area also offers short hiking trails and picnic areas. It's a great place to introduce yourself to the Bitterroot's native birds and other species.

The Teller Wildlife Refuge is a unique, private wildlife refuge consisting of 1,100 acres of riverside property near Corvallis. The Teller, too, is home to species ranging from beaver and porcupine to herons and hawks. The Teller Wildlife Refuge offers environmental education programs to valley youth, and is available for hikers as well.

Climb a bit higher and you may hear pikas in the rockslides, or porcupines munching on the lodgepole pines. Elk retreat to the higher forests during hunting season, only to reappear tantalizingly close in the spring, cropping the bunch grasses on open, south-facing slopes – or brazenly poaching hay in open pastures.

Those elk represent a Bitterroot kind of success story. Although healthy elk herds exist on both sides of the valley today, they had been hunted to the point of scarcity early in this century. Sportsmen belatedly became alarmed, and began a "subscription campaign" in the valley that raised the money to transplant a herd of elk from Yellowstone in 1912. The descendants of that herd, which mixed with the last wily stragglers of the original stock, produce the bugling serenade that defines September for those who frequent the woods in that month.

Mountain bison and antelope, too, once inhabited the Bitterroot, but never in great numbers, and not at all since the valley was first settled. No efforts have been made to re-introduce them.

The great predators of the Northern Rockies, the gray wolf and the grizzly bear, were systematically eliminated by the early settlers, the last grizzlies being hunted in the 1920's and 1930's. They are now making a tenuous comeback, with wolves re-introduced in the early 1990's in the Frank Church/River of No Return wilderness in Idaho, migrating quickly to the Selway-Bitterroot Wilderness, and now making appearances in the valley. The Selway also yields rare, credible grizzly sightings, though none are positively confirmed. Grizzly re-introduction is a hotly-debated topic in the Bitterroot, but the animals may someday take care of it

themselves, with or without human intervention.

One other great predator continues to thrive in the Bitterroot – the mountain lion, or cougar. Lions are generally secretive animals, preying primarily on deer. As development along the forest edge has brought more people to live in deer habitat, however, so has it brought them into cat habitat. Likewise, as burgeoning deer populations have caused them to appear on the edge of town, so have they drawn the cats in close. Conflicts between people and mountain lions remain rare, but people outdoors anywhere in the valley should be aware of the possibility.

Bird lovers will delight at some of the lovely and rare species to be found here, numbering close to 250 in all. Colorful western tanagers join lazuli buntings and pine grosbeaks at feeders. Several species of hummingbirds arrive each spring to sip nectar from the valley's innumerable feeders. The extra-large pileated woodpecker joins a handful of smaller species down to nuthatches in clinging to the bark of the valley's trees. At the top of the chain, peregrine falcons are now successfully established in several canyon eyries, while bald and golden eagles are seasonal visitors, along with a healthy population of osprey along the river.

Game birds in the valley include ringneck pheasants, several species of grouse, chukars, mourning doves and wild turkeys.

Finally, the Bitterroot River and its tributaries comprise a highly productive "blue ribbon" fishery – with occasional barren stretches due to irrigation and logging. Native trout and introduced species have reached an uneasy standoff, but at any time the delicate balance can tip. Already, high in the watershed, the native bull trout are in serious decline due to degradation of water quality, while down in the lower Bitterroot River, voracious pike (an introduced species) are changing the species balance. Whirling disease, which affects primarily rainbow trout, is another factor in this equation, although the Bitterroot has so far escaped serious infection.

Fishing on the river is managed by segments, some of it catch-and-release only for certain species, some of it closed to certain species. The aim is to maintain a fishery of native trout – cutthroat and bull trout in particular. At this time, the river is not stocked with hatchery fish at all, although Lake Como receives a batch of rainbows annually.

While the introduced species such as brown trout, rainbows, and brook trout compete with the natives for survival, the anglers don't seem to mind hooking them. On the other hand, whitefish and suckers also populate the river, but are not as popular with the rod-and-reel set.

The streams feeding the Bitterroot are keys to the strength of the fishery, but the lower reaches of many are almost completely dried up (we politely say "dewatered") by irrigation demands in late summer. Others suffer severe siltation as a result of logging and the associated road-building. Consequently, wildlife biologists are working with citizen groups like Trout Unlimited to protect and improve trout habitat in the watershed.

mann spruce and subalpine fir coexist on moist, higher-altitude sites. The cones
spruce are pendant, hanging down, while the cones of any true fir are
ctively upright, and disintegrate when they ripen. (R. Lawrence photo)

A Famous Recluse

Under the heading of wildlife it is fair to note that while nobody has claimed to see Bigfoot or Sasquatch in the Bitterroots, there have been a number of individuals who have chosen to live for various periods of time in the area's vast wilderness. These include the Ridgerunner, a famous recluse who lived in the Bitterroot mountains for twenty-four years, notorious for breaking into cabins to steal food, leaving behind a collection of half-emptied cans and a pile of dirty dishes.

The mentally unbalanced recluse turned out to be Bill Moreland, who lived in the wild from 1936 until he was first captured in 1945 after becoming too great a nuisance for the Forest Service to ignore. A sympathetic judge turned him loose after ninety days in captivity, and he went back to his old ways.

It wasn't until he developed the bad habit of shooting at people (inaccurately, as it turned out) that he was re-captured in 1958 and committed to an asylum...from which he escaped the next year. He finally retired from cabin-raiding in 1960, and spent the rest of his life in a mental institution.

NATURE TRAILS

Hike one of the valley's self-guided nature trails to learn more about the natural history of the area. The Forest Service offers the Charles Waters Nature Trail, the Larry Creek Fire Ecology Trail, the Willoughby Environmental Education Area Nature Trail, and the Centennial Grove Nature Trail. The Lee Metcalf National Wildlife Refuge has a self-guided walk, and the Teller Wildlife Refuge offers environmental education programs. Contact the appropriate agency for more information.

ll, sheer-faced spires of Blodgett Canyon are a result of glaciation. Besides obvious scenic attractions, they also offer a variety of challenges for rock ers. (R. Lawrence photo)

Indian Summer brings out the extravagant colors and moods of the Bitterroot. Crisp mornings, warm days, and swift nightfall mark the season's change.

ed specimens dot the ridgelines of the high Bitterroots, attesting to the harsh ions in which they grow. It may take hundreds of years for a tree to mature, and is likewise slowed. (R. Lawrence photo)

*, and highly visible on dry hillsides, *leaf balsamroot is a welcome sight *it blooms in early spring.

*vy snow leaves picnickers out of luck, but birds, squirrels and deer will *bly all find their way to the feeder before evening falls. (R. Lawrence photo)

Seasons in the Bitterroot frequently overlap. Here, fall colors arrive in late summer, as a hillside dries out.

A mountain lake, the perfect place for undisturbed, reflective moments. Barbara June)

hellebore commonly grows in high, moist,
pine meadows. It has some medicinal uses, but
sonous in larger doses.

en Darby and Stevensville the channel of the Bitterroot River becomes braided,
xbows and sloughs a common testament to its capacity for change.

A full moon illuminates the dry east-side foothills, where pungent juniper and sagebrush flavor the evening breeze.

Waterfalls grace many of the westside canyons, delighting hikers–and in many defining exactly how far upstream you'll find fish.

More than one person has found that a rainbow arching over the valley doesn't lead to the pot of gold, it IS the pot of gold. Scenic splendor is a wealth we share daily.

in high mountain meadows are spongy, absorbing water as the snow goes off,
y releasing it through the summer, nurturing a community of wildflowers and
ure-loving plants. (Dale Burk photo)

Mule deer have been retreating from some of their historic range as whitetail deer encroach. Changes in hunting regulations have helped their numbers to rebound somewhat in recent years.

The only owl equipped with a back-up warning: the pygmy owl's call is typic single note repeated 60-80 times a minute, sounding like the beeper on equipment in reverse gear.

The pika, (also known as a "rock rabbit), busies itself in rocky, high mountain habitat, gathering food to last it through the long, frigid winters. Hikers commonly hear its high-pitched "eek" echoing in alpine cirques. (R. Lawrence photo)

ider the raven the smartest bird in the forest. Playful and inventive, its niche as
venger inclines it toward success in hard times as well as good. In this sense, the
(and its equally raucous relative, the magpie) resembles many Bitterrooters.

...and bobcat, closely related, keep the rodents and lagomorphs (rabbits and ...) on guard.

Bitterrooters are deeply divided over whether, and how, the grizzly bear should be re-introduced to the Selway-Bitterroot Wilderness. The last of the great bears living in the area was killed in the 1930's, leaving vacant its undisputed spot at the top of the food chain. Ideally, a couple of discreet bears will sneak, unnoticed, into the wilderness and quietly set up housekeeping while every human in the county is engaged in arguing about the government's role in their return.

...are more likely to hear the Great Horned Owl than to see it, but these ...ificent birds are not uncommon in the Bitterroot. Capable of taking prey up to ...ze of cats and small dogs, they more commonly prey on smaller rodents. (Photo ...ira June)

When it's getting too hot in the valley, it's just right for a hike in the whitebar
forests found high in the Bitterroots. Spring-like conditions may persist into A
with abundant wildflowers and cool daytime temperatures. Bring your jacket.
Burk photo)

Northern grey wolves, re-introduced in Idaho, have moved into the Selway-Bitterroot
Wilderness, and make occasional appearances in the valley. They are a protected
species, and many local ranchers and other landowners have cooperated in allowing
individuals and packs to roam the valley's fringe.

The largest bird you're likely to see in the Bitterroot, (or anywhere else, for that matter): the Sandhill Crane. It can be distinguished from the Great Blue Heron in flight by the fact that its neck is extended, where the heron's head is distinctively tucked back. (Photo Barbara June)

country horsemen push the season a bit, getting into the high country just as the snowshoers are leaving. Adventurous souls use this alpine wilderness in every on, but rarely have to share it except during the six weeks that pass for summer eline and above. (Dale Burk photo)

Lupine is a member of the pea family, blooming in late spring/early summer.

Hayfields and pastures occupy many of the fertile valley bottoms. Deer and elk frequently sift down from the cover of the coulees by night to take advantage of the free munchies.

A river otter warily dines al fresco on a very fresh fish.

Wildfire! After a hundred years of strenuous fire suppression, the many roles of fire are only now appreciated. It clears out decadent forest growth, but it also destroys valuable timber and homes; it recycles forest nutrients, but it can also sterilize soils and lead to erosion. The forests of the Northern Rockies are adapted to periodic wildfires, but as more homes are built along the forest edge, the potential for a costly disaster increases.

Grey Jays, more commonly known as "camp robbers," are not shy about their intentions. Leave food unattended on your picnic table at your peril. (R. Lawrence photo)

Turkeys, once an unlikely sight in the Bitterroot, are now thriving in some of the valley's open woodlands. Listen for their distinctive gobbling early in the morning. You'll know it when you hear it.

Waiting for you to drop a crumb or two from your picnic, this chipmunk keeps cool in the shade of a cottonwood. (Photo Barbara June)

First to catch the morning's light, last to relinquish it at night, the high peaks of the Bitterroot Range draw a cottony cloak about them.

Everybody in the Bitterroot has a bear story. Black bears are numerous along the urban/forest interface, and occasionally in town. Having garbage cans, fruit trees, or beehives makes you a target for a raid. Black bears are seldom aggressive toward humans, but should always be treated with respect.

PART TWO: HISTORY

THE BITTERROOT SALISH

The history of the Bitterroot valley prior to the 19th century is sketchy, difficult to piece together. Archaeologists haven't found much direct evidence of prehistoric occupation in the valley, save for a handful of pictographs and a few sites yielding ancient artifacts, most notably around Lake Como.

Those who want to understand the history of the area prior to first contact with whites in the early 1800's have two resources: the records left in the form of physical artifacts–tools, bones, pictographs, and so forth – and the tribal traditions of the Native Americans who lived here, handed down through stories. Scientists have even drawn some climate data from various sources, including analysis of pollen deposits in a bog at Lost Trail Pass.

Dating physical evidence, though, and then trying to draw accurate conclusions about the people who left it, is not always significantly more accurate than interpreting the oral traditions handed down within a tribe – and often these two sources conflict. Because of that, little of what follows can be asserted as solid fact.

Historians have a bit more to go on if they look at the regional picture. According to the best evidence, the first native peoples may have arrived in western Montana 14,000 years ago, and were certainly in place by 9,000 B.C., after the last emptying of glacial Lake Missoula. The region was hot and arid, populated by small groups of mobile foragers. No evidence indicates that these first individuals had any kind of tribal identity, or that they were permanent, year-round residents. About 4,000 years ago, though, the natives of this area adopted a common, seasonal lifestyle – harvesting roots and greens early in the year, gathering berries in the summer and hunting in the fall, before returning to winter camps.

These ancient inhabitants are now identified by anthropologists as part of the "Plateau Culture." It was distinct from the surrounding cultures – the Plains Culture to the east, the Coastal Culture of the Pacific coast, the Shoshone or Great Basin Culture to the south and the Boreal peoples of the north – but they all influenced one another in various ways. Climatic changes during this period also influenced them, as forest cover advanced and retreated.

Let's clear up some terminology, at least for the purpose of this book – writers and historians are notoriously inconsistent about the use of tribal names. The Indians who called this area home were of the Salish stock. "Salish" now refers broadly to the many tribes of the Plateau whose language is derived from the Salishan root. "Flathead" is how Lewis & Clark referred to the people living specifically in the Bitterroot, and that is how most writers have referred to them since, although the name has also been applied to other groups. (The Flatheads of western Montana didn't practice head flattening, but the Indian's sign-language symbol for them was two hands placed flat against the temples). At one time or another, the Bitterroot

Valley has probably been used by numerous bands or groups, including the Pend d'Oreilles, Flathead, Nez Perce, and Shoshone. Others no doubt traveled through it or knew of it.

To avoid confusion, the people living in this valley at the time of Lewis & Clark's arrival will be called the Bitterroot Salish.

Sometime after 1300 A.D., tribal identities became more distinct among the peoples of the Plateau. The Bitterroot Salish were joined in western Montana by other branches of the Salish, and by the Kootenai tribe. The latter had a language unrelated to the Salish, but were geographically close and on friendly terms. Various accounts show the Bitterroot Valley occupied by the Pend d'Oreilles or the Flatheads at one time or another, and most agree that the Flathead "territory" extended onto the Montana plains at least as far as the Three Forks area.

What they had in common, but differentiated them from other Salish groups, was the absence of salmon from their yearly diet.

As long ago as 2,500 B.C., they were using the high mountains of the Bitterroots to harvest whitebark pine nuts. Their diet was highly varied, and included big game (bison, elk, deer, and bighorn sheep, primarily), roots, berries, herbs and fish. Bitterroots were harvested on drier ridges, and the important camas roots were dug in wet areas. Lake Como, before it was dammed early in the 1900's, consisted of a shallow lake, sometimes noted as two ponds connected by wetlands, where camas grew in abundance, making it an important site for hungry foragers.

Because their range extended beyond the continental divide, these people were among the few Indians who were adept at living both in the mountains as well as on the plains.

Some historians assert that the Bitterroot Salish knew the Bitterroot River as the Red Willow, rendering it as "Ootlashoot" in their tongue. Lewis & Clark recorded the term, applying it to the tribe as well. Others contend that the Salish name for the river is the more literal "Spitlem Seukn," or "water of the bitter root," and the valley is called "Spitlemen," for "place of the bitter root" (phonetic spellings differ).

Whatever they called it, the people living here developed traditions of their own, and annual rituals including the digging of bitterroots and camas roots in May and June, and migrations to the plains to hunt bison in the fall. Their spirituality included respect for all living beings, and they were rewarded with a good life lived in a place that offered everything they needed.

Boys would go on solo vision quests to seek a spirit guide, usually an animal spirit, but not necessarily. Both Kootenai canyon and the butte east of Corvallis (decorated now with the letter "C") were sites used for such sojourns. Girls might undertake such quests, but would be accompanied.

Their oral tradition was rich in stories, told to children by their grandparents, about Coyote and others. The tribes of the region all believed themselves to be the sons and daughters of Coyote, a tricky being who figured prominently in many of their stories. The Bitterroot Salish also told of the Foolish People, a race of dwarves, dirty and stupid, who were said to have inhabited the valley before the arrival of the Salish.

The Medicine Tree, south of Darby, was a Ponderosa pine in which a ram's skull was embedded. The local legend told how coyote had tricked the ram into entangling his horns there, the moral of the story being the triumph of wit over strength. The tree earned the status of a sacred site, where offerings might be left to procure favors from the spirits.

Shamans and magicians looked after the people in many capacities–shamans, in particular, were frequently called upon to help locate lost items.

Two episodes of vast importance changed their existence completely. First, probably sometime around 1730, the tribe obtained horses. The Bitterroot provided great pasture for their animals, which was a mixed blessing, as it made it a more desirable place–for everyone. Horses gave the Bitterroot Salish much greater mobility, but it had the same effect for their enemies, as well. The Blackfeet probably got both horses and firearms somewhat earlier than the Salish, and exercised their much greater power over them, making their visits to the buffalo country of the plains a much more dangerous affair. They also raided the valley to steal horses.

The greater mobility led to larger confederations. By 1800 the disparate bands of Flatheads were united, largely in response to raids by tribes of the Blackfoot Confederation from the north, and the Shoshone from the south.

The second event of disastrous significance was a regional smallpox epidemic among the tribes of the Northwest that left them devastated. From 1760-70 the disease raged, sweeping up the Missouri River, then flaring again in 1781. Nobody can say for sure what proportion of the Indians died in that time, but the consensus is just under half, with some estimates ranging up to as much as two-thirds. Some hard-hit

Undated photo of an unnamed Salish Indian, probably taken in the late 1800's, with St. Mary's Peak in the background. (BRVHS Photo)

bands disappeared entirely. Compounding these events were the rumors of white people appearing in the region. Certainly, trade goods began to filter into the region. Fur traders and trappers were in contact with the Blackfoot of the north, and British ships began visiting the west coast in 1774.

The culture that Lewis and Clark encountered was a culture reeling from several strong jolts.

It is important to re-emphasize that the Bitterroot's history doesn't begin with the arrival of Lewis and Clark in 1805. This valley was inhabited by a people with a rich culture and history, who had lived here for generations, and who expected to continue to do so for generations to come. Their way of life was well-adapted to the conditions here, and they had well-established relations with other tribal groups in the Northwest.

The conceit that Lewis & Clark "discovered" this place is a grave insult to those who had known it as home for years untold.

LEWIS & CLARK

The Lewis and Clark Expedition arrived in the Bitterroot Valley in September of 1805. They had made a difficult crossing over what is now known as Lost Trail Pass from Idaho, and were spotted by a chieftain known as Three Eagles. He and others greeted them at Ross's Hole, near Sula, the first contact between whites and the Salish Indians (variously recorded by the explorers as the Oot-lash-shoots, Tushepau and Flatheads).

The Salish initially had no idea how to deal with these intruders. The bedraggled Corps of Discovery, recently thrashed by their crossing of Lost Trail Pass, didn't appear to be a war party, especially as it included a woman and an infant. Clark's black slave, York, was an utter mystery. Some warriors blackened themselves with charcoal for various purposes, but his appearance must have been perplexing. The men weren't carrying blankets, which could either indicate a fast-moving war party, or a party so poor they had none. The combination of York, Sacagawea and her son probably predisposed the Salish to greet these strangers cautiously, but more cordially than they might otherwise.

The explorers quickly observed that these people spoke a language unrelated to that of the plains and interior tribes they had so far been dealing with, and this, as much as any hints of geography, confirmed that they had reached the Pacific provinces.

In Clark's description of the event (in his atrocious spelling), the expedition *"prosued our Course down the Creek to the forks about 5 miles where we met a part of the Tushepau nation, of 33 Lodges about 80 men 400 Total and at least 500 horses, those people recved us friendly, threw white robes over out Sholders & Smoked in the pipes of peace, we encamped with them and found them friendly . . . I was the first white man who ever wer on the waters of this river."*

The explorers traded for 29 *"elegant"* horses, pack animals they needed and which Clarke forebodingly noted would be useful *"to eate, if necessary."* These horses proved absolutely critical to their success in getting over the mountains ahead. They also received food, robes, and saddles.

The party then proceeded northward down the valley. Lewis reported that *"the country in the valley of this river is generally a prairie and from five to 6 miles wide."* The river, he found, *"is here a handsome stream about 100 yards wide and affords a considerable quantity of very clear water."*

The expedition descended the length of the valley from Ross' Hole to Lolo so quickly you'd think they were being chased. Their enemy, they knew, was time, and the approach of winter.

Leaving Ross' Hole on September 6 they crossed a low mountain rather than follow the river through a narrow, difficult canyon, then descended Spring gulch to regain the river, where they camped not far below Sula. They then moved downriver to the confluence of the east and west forks, the Bitterroot's true headwaters, and continued on the west side of the river until Old Toby, their guide, convinced them to ford the stream once again to gain better forage for their stock. They camped that night about a mile above Sleeping Child creek, where they ravenously partook of the bounty their hunters finally succeeded in bringing down.

On September 8 they made good time, descending the valley on the east side, crossing Skalkaho creek and several others, probably lunching on the banks of Willow creek, before camping just south of the present site of Stevensville. (The present Eastside Highway follows their route fairly closely). Early snow had topped the Bitterroots, and every member of the party was particularly aware that to pursue their route, they had to cross those mountains somehow. They must have seemed a most formidable obstacle, and every surviving journal reveals a party continually glancing over their left shoulders at those imposing, snow-clad summits.

The following day they shouldered their loads, which now must have included some doubts, and continued down the valley on the east side, crossing the river north of Florence and proceeding to a camp on the south bank of Lolo creek about a mile and a half from its mouth. This camp they called *"Travelers' Rest Camp,"* and they remained there for two nights.

When the horses and men were rested, they turned west up Lolo creek. The epic crossing of the Bitterroot range that followed, over Lolo pass to the Clearwater river, was the most difficult part of their entire journey.

Startling News At Traveler's Rest

It was at Traveler's Rest that the Lewis & Clark party heard the startling news that a route existed that would take them from where they stood to the Missouri River above the Gates of the Mountains in about four days. Their own route, ascending the Missouri to its source, dropping over Lemhi pass into Idaho, then crossing back into Montana at Lost Trail pass, had taken them a bit more than seven weeks of hard traveling.

Not surprisingly, on their return from the Pacific in 1806, Lewis elected to explore this new – and much shorter – route. Starting on July 4th, his party moved from present-day Lolo north to the Missoula valley, then followed the Blackfoot river to its headwaters, crossing over the Rocky Mountains at what is now known as Lewis & Clark pass (although Clark never saw it). They took five days in the crossing.

Crossing the Bitterroot range between September 11, 1805, and September 16, Lewis made the following observations:

"The road through this hilly country is very bad, passing over hills and

through steep hollows, over falling timber, etc. . . . most intolerable road on the sides of the steep, stony mountains . . . thickly covered with undergrowth and falling timber . . . party and horses much fatigued . . . in the valleys it rained and hailed, on top of the mountains some snow fell . . . we were compelled to kill a colt for our men and ourselves to eat for the want of meat . . . the mountains which we passed today much worse than yesterday, the last excessively bad and thickly strewed with falling timber . . . several horses slipped and rolled down steep hills which hurt them very much . . . two of our horses gave out, poor and too much hurt to proceed on . . . began to snow today . . . I have been wet and as cold in every part as I ever was in my life . . . to describe the road today would be a repetition of yesterday except the snow which made it much worse."

On their return from the mouth of the Columbia in 1806, they were forced to delay their crossing of Lolo Pass until late June due to snow that lay ten feet deep. In fact, the only time they were forced to retrace their steps on the entire expedition occurred as they retreated from their first attempt on the pass. Their crossing was made even more difficult by the swollen creeks, full of icy runoff, and by a lack of forage for their horses. They followed the trail by looking for trees that the Indians had peeled to eat the inner bark, as food was scarce.

Once across the pass they descended Lolo creek and camped at Lolo Hot Springs, where one can image how much pleasure the men and their Indian guides derived from bathing in the warm waters. Clark reported that the Indians amused themselves by jumping from the hot water into the icy creek, remaining as long as they could bear it, then returning to the hot springs.

The next day they reported traveling 13 miles, entirely over packed snow, and found that the inconvenience of slipping was more than made up for by the easy passage it provided for them over the rocks and fallen logs that had bedeviled them on their westward course. The next day found them encamped once again at the confluence of Lolo Creek with the Bitterroot River, "Traveler's Rest." They remained for three days this time, putting their equipment in order, and enjoying evenings full of horse races and foot races against the Nez Perce who had accompanied them over the pass.

The captains, meanwhile, were refining their plan to divide the expedition at this point. Nine men were to go with Lewis, pass through the Missoula valley, then ascend the Blackfoot river and cross the Continental Divide at what is now known as Lewis & Clark Pass (even though Clark never saw it).

They split up on July 3, as emotional a leave-taking as one can imagine. The following day Lewis celebrated Independence Day with an inadvertent, mile and a half trip down the Clark Fork River as they attempted to cross its runoff-swollen waters on a cobbled-together raft. As they tried to land, he was swept off by an overhanging bush and forced to swim ashore.

Lewis and his party then made their way uneventfully east to the Great Falls of the Missouri, and eventually downriver from there, surviving a scrape with the Blackfeet on the Marias River.

Captain Clark took the remainder of the party back up the Bitterroot valley, leaving Travelers' Rest on July 3. They once again made excellent time, lunching near Kootenai creek and camping that night on Blodgett creek, just outside the site of present-day Hamilton. They celebrated the Fourth of July, 1806, by traveling another thirty miles overland on the west side of the valley, camping on the West Fork. This rapid progress is all the more impressive as the going would have been easier on the east side, with better forage as well, but the river remained too high for them to ford.

The next day they forded the swollen West Fork, and the East Fork as well, continuing upstream past Ross' Hole and camping near what is now the Sula Ranger Station. After a frosty night, they diverged from their route of the previous year, instead following an Indian trail that angled up and crossed the Continental Divide at Gibbons Pass, eventually leading them into the Big Hole valley, and once again to the headwaters of the Missouri, where Sacagawea was able to serve as a guide.

Clark's group passed the hot springs at Jackson, in the Big Hole, and continued to Camp Fortunate on the banks of the Beaverhead, where they had buried their cache of goods–in particular, their tobacco, which the men eagerly dug up, before attending to the unearthing of their boats.

They proceeded to the Three Forks area, from which point (after further dividing the party), Clark's men eventually reached the Yellowstone river, which they descended to a successful rendezvous with Lewis just below the confluence of the Yellowstone and Missouri.

One intriguing consequence of Clark's passage through the valley is the strong possibility that he fathered a son, either by a Salish or Nez Perce woman, while here. Records refer to a Peter Clarke (sic), reputedly baptized after the coming of the missionaries, and his son Zachariah, which was generally rendered as "Sacalee" Clarke (sic), both of whom lived among the Salish.

THE FUR TRAPPER ERA

Over the next thirty years, few other whites laid eyes on the valley, but of those few who did many are famous names from the fur trade era.

The great Canadian explorer and trader David Thompson was the first man to map and explore the headwaters of the Columbia river, and descended its length shortly after Lewis & Clark. On a subsequent trip he scanned the Bitterroot valley from the top of Missoula's Mount Jumbo in 1812, before returning to his winter headquarters on the lower Clark Fork. The Salish, he recorded, were a "fine race of moral Indians."

Ten years later Michel Bourdon led a trapping party into the Bitterroot valley, and the following year Finan McDonald brought a company of 65 trappers through the valley, no doubt providing a startling spectacle for the local Salish.

In 1824 Alexander Ross, a fur trader for the Pacific Fur Company, led a trapping expedition from the Flathead river to the Snake river country, departing in February of that year. The large party, containing 55 men of numerous nationalities, 25 women and 64 children, moved slowly up the Bitterroot valley, arriving in the area now known as Ross's Hole, near present-day Sula, on March 12. There they found their way to the Big Hole blocked by impassably deep snow.

Ross called it the "Valley of Troubles," owing to his having to spend a miserable month there while the party tried to force a trail through the snow. He finally succeeded in getting his unruly troupe over Gibbons Pass and on their way, returning via the same route in November of that year.

In the next few years a handful of notables traversed the valley, including mountain men Jedediah Smith, Joe Meek, Tom Fitzpatrick, and Kit Carson, the latter much better known for his exploits in the southern Rockies.

Significantly, many of the early trappers, in Ross's party and others, were Indians of the Iroquois nation, originally from the eastern woodlands of the U.S. and Canada. The beaver in their part of the country had been largely trapped-out, and these experienced trappers were recruited by the Canadians to travel out West where beaver were still abundant. The native Piegan and Blackfeet had shown little inclination to trap beaver, preferring to hunt buffalo, so the Iroquois joined many important early trapping parties.

THE COMING OF THE BLACK ROBES – ST. MARY'S MISSION

By 1824 a dozen of those Iroquois Indians had elected to remain in the Bitterroot valley, and were accepted among the Salish, marrying into the tribe. One of those who came to share the valley with the Salish was Big Ignace LaMousse, an Iroquois who may have found his way to the Bitterroot valley sometime prior to 1820.

St. Mary's Mission is the simple, rough-hewn symbol of early white settlement in the valley. Established in 1841 at the persistent request of the valley's Indian population (and rebuilt 25 years later), it now stands watch over a valley from which those original inhabitants were expelled.

Big Ignace was a baptized Christian, and he spoke of this new faith to the Salish, teaching them the Lord's Prayer and the rudiments of the faith.

Some records tell of Shining Shirt, a member of the tribe, who is said to have had a vision of the white men in black robes, bringing strong medicine to the tribe.

The Salish were impressed by Big Ignace's faith, and possibly by the idea that this superior new religion would give them an advantage in battle over their enemies. So desperately did they wish to embrace it that in 1831, four young Indians, one Salish and three Nez Perce, mounted up and traveled, incredibly, to St. Louis, to petition for a priest, a so-called "black robe," to come live among them.

This remarkable trip took the devout foursome 1,800 miles overland or by river, without roads or maps, through hostile, unknown territory. They arrived at the cathedral in St. Louis in October of 1831 and communicated their wishes in sign language, the only means they had of conversing with the French missionaries.

The riders had worn themselves out on their journey, and two of the young men died within a month of their arrival, and their deaths and burials were recorded in the parish records in St. Louis. The other two wintered there but were unable to persuade the missionaries to dispatch a priest. According to church records, they set out for home the following spring, but were never heard from again.

Three years later, Insula, a Flathead, arrived at the Green River Rendezvous to try to solicit a visit from the black robes. Instead, he encountered Dr. Marcus Whitman, a Presbyterian who would later play a role in the settlement of eastern Washington. The Protestant Whitman appeared to Insula to lack the potent medicine of the Jesuits, so he didn't pursue his help. Whitman's partner, the Rev. Samuel Parker, appears to have traveled up the West Fork in September of 1835 in the company of a band of Nez Perce, but the Salish weren't interested.

Meanwhile, frustrated at having heard nothing from the unlucky riders of the 1831 party, Big Ignace himself set out for St. Louis with two of his sons. They, too, arrived safely in the river town, and spent a winter among others of the Iroquois nation who had settled in the area. After baptizing Ignace's sons, Church officials in St. Louis relented, agreeing to send a priest, and a satisfied Big Ignace returned to the Bitterroot valley in 1836.

When no priest appeared, though, the indefatigable Big Ignace LaMousse undertook yet another trip to the Catholic fathers in St. Louis in 1837. He and his party, once again including both Salish and Nez Perce, were surprised by a band of hostile Sioux, and slain along the Platte river in Wyoming.

Instead of giving up the quest, and spurred by a smallpox epidemic that struck their camp in 1838, Young Ignace LaMousse, very much his father's son, took a friend, Peter Gaucher, and undertook his own pilgrimage to St. Louis in 1839. En route, they chanced upon Father Pierre-Jean DeSmet at his cabin near Council Bluffs, Iowa. The history of the west is peppered with magnificent coincidences, and this is one of them.

Father DeSmet was just embarking on a career that would take him all over the West, and after meeting the twosome from the Bitterroot he quickly obtained the bishop's permission for a survey mission to the Salish. Over the winter the Belgian Jesuit raised the funds for his project, and ultimately began trekking westward in the spring of 1840, in the company of Young Ignace. (Peter Gaucher, himself no slouch,

Father Pierre Jean DeSmet, whose chance encounter with a delegation of Indians from the Bitterroot Valley led directly to the establishment of St. Mary's Mission. (BRVHS Photo)

had already returned, alone, to the valley.)

DeSmet, traveling in the company of trappers, celebrated the first Catholic Mass in this region on Sunday, July 5, at Green River, with parts spoken in French, English, Latin, Salish and Snake. He spent a summer in Idaho and Montana without ever reaching the Bitterroot Valley, returning to St. Louis later that year. He convinced his superiors of the need for a permanent mission in the Bitterroot, and they concurred. Finally, on September 24, 1841, DeSmet, in the company of two priests, Fr. Gregory Mengarini and Fr. Nicolas Point, and three lay brothers, arrived in the valley to begin construction of a mission, 25 by 33 feet, which he christened "St. Mary's."

St. Mary's Mission was raised near the main Salish encampment in the Bitterroot valley, near what is now Stevensville. Built of cottonwood logs and plastered with clay, it became the center of the first permanent settlement in what is now the state of Montana. The mission church known as St. Mary's is a monument to the determination of the Indians who risked their lives many times over to obtain the services of a priest.

ST. MARY'S MISSION AND FORT OWEN

The history of white settlement in Montana begins with St. Mary's mission. (DeSmet also gave the name to the peak and to the river, although the latter failed to take). St. Mary's was not the first fort or trading post in what is now Montana, but it was the first to take root permanently. Some other significant Montana "firsts"

associated with the mission:
- their three carts and a wagon were the first wheeled vehicles in the valley
- first use of irrigation
- first wheat (and other grains) grown
- first flour ground
- first logs sawn
- first Doctor's office and drug dispensary
- first domestic livestock (cattle, swine and poultry)

It would be difficult to guess how many other "firsts" are associated with the mission, and its last chapter has yet to be written. Modern Montana, however, took root in the soil of the Bitterroot valley in September of 1841 and its first fruit was a small church enclosing 825 square feet.

The mission at St. Mary's slowly began to draw to it the elements of a self-sustaining community. The Jesuits built a flour mill and a sawmill, and planted an orchard and various crops. They devised a simple irrigation system to sustain the crops through the arid summer. They shared their harvests with their Salish congregation, and in turn the Salish shared their standard fare of dried meats, dried roots and berries, and herbs.

Arriving at St. Mary's in 1845 was Father Antony Ravalli, a 33-year-old Italian recruited for missionary work by Father DeSmet while on a European tour. Father Ravalli had a working knowledge of medicine and pharmacology, and quickly acquired other skills necessary to survive on the frontier. Father Ravalli would come to play an important role in the future of St. Mary's.

Father Antony Ravalli

Father Antony Ravalli was born May 16, 1812 in Ferrara, northern Italy. He was a gifted student who chose to join the Jesuit order in 1827, taking his final vows while en route from Antwerp, Belgium, to Fort Vancouver in 1843, appropriately enough aboard a ship called the "Indefatigable." By the time he came to the United States with Father DeSmet in that year, his talents and knowledge encompassed not just medicine and theology, but most of the natural sciences and an acquaintance with engineering and agronomy as well. He was conversant in literature and skilled in the arts, and in fact carved the altar and many of the adornments at the mission church, and his paintings hung on the walls. Described as tall and portly, he was an ingenious man who could fashion a sawmill from wagon wheels or distill alcohol from camas roots, when not teaching the catechism.

When he arrived in the United States he was posted first to Fort Colville, in Washington, then transferred to St. Mary's in 1845. He remained there until it was closed in 1850, then returned in 1866 to build the new mission, which still stands. Among his other legacies are the name of Lake Como, which he named for the lake of similar beauty in northern Italy, and, of course, Ravalli County, which was named for the dauntless Italian Jesuit who made the Bitterroot his home.

The missionaries taught the Salish to tend crops, and for a time the Indians seemed willing to give up their old ways for the new, in exchange for the strong new medicine the black robes' faith conveyed. Father Mengarini became quite fluent in Salish, and began to compile a grammar. The Indians' conversion may never have been whole-hearted, though. They still rode off to the plains of eastern Montana to hunt the buffalo, and when word got out that Father DeSmet aimed to baptize their blood enemies the Blackfeet, who dominated their hunting grounds, the Salish became somewhat testy. The possibility that the Blackfeet might receive this same "medicine" was a great concern.

Meanwhile, the promise of prime buffalo hides soon brought traders to the area. The foremost of these traders was John Owen. By 1850, the fortunes of St. Mary's mission had reversed almost entirely. Some of the traders had introduced whiskey to the Salish, and for various reasons (including the whiskey) many of the Salish were falling away from the church. Continuing depredations by the Blackfeet had a demoralizing effect, and the Jesuits felt it would be prudent to suspend their mission for a time, concentrating their efforts elsewhere.

To that end, Father Joset of St. Mary's was authorized to sell the church's properties there to John Owen. The deal was closed on Nov. 5, 1850, for $250 – the first legal transaction recorded in Montana.

FORT OWEN

Owen soon moved his operations from the mission building to a new trading post he built a short distance to the north, modestly christening it "Fort Owen." (Two years later, the Jesuits requested that he burn the church, to prevent its desecration). Surrounded by a gated stockade, his "fort" did indeed afford some protection from the occasional raid, but it never actually served as a military outpost. Owen himself was

St. Mary's Mission celebrates its 100th Birthday, during the 1941 Creamery Picnic in Stevensville. (BRVHS Photo)

accorded the honorary title of "Major," but only for his services as a civilian sutler and later as an Indian agent, rather than for any military service.

Fort Owen grew from a few rude structures surrounded by log palisades to encompass a double row of adobe buildings, enclosed by adobe walls and guarded by bastions at the southern corners. There Owen conducted his trading, maintained the Flathead Indian Agency, and had his own personal quarters where he lived with his wife Nancy, a Shoshone Indian.

In its time, Fort Owen saw the arrival of dozens of significant figures in early Montana history, civilian and military alike. After the conclusion of the Hellgate Treaty of 1855, it also became the anchor for the community that would become Stevensville, in spite of the fact the land still belonged to the Salish.

Major Owen operated his post from 1850 until its sale on Dec. 30, 1872. Its fortunes surged and ebbed, but though it afforded him and Nancy a relatively comfortable living, it never made him rich. Still, he lived well and entertained as grandly as circumstances might permit in those times. Visitors always received an enthusiastic welcome, and many wrote of the (relatively) lavish accommodations they were afforded at Fort Owen.

In 1856 Owen was appointed as an agent of the Indian Bureau, a post in which he served for six years. It must have been with mixed feelings that he observed the flow of settlers into the area, which the settlers felt had been opened by the Hellgate Treaty of 1855, but the Salish rightly believed was still theirs. As Indian Agent, he was obliged to represent their interests, but as a trader, he couldn't help but appreciate

Salish Indians participated in the centennial celebration of St. Mary's Mission at the 1941 Creamery Picnic. (BRVHS Photo)

the added business.

In 1865 Owen opened a large grist mill, but his grand vision of Fort Owen as the trading center of western Montana had already eluded him.

By the early 1860's the village of Hell Gate (soon to be known as Missoula) was firmly established, and its superior position along the east-west Mullan Road (completed the previous year) gave it an unsurpassable advantage. The Mullan Road connected the gold fields of Montana to the ports of the Columbia river and the west coast. Hell Gate, positioned astride that road, quickly became the dominant community in western Montana.

The first territorial legislature met in 1865, and passed over Fort Owen for the county seat, favoring Hell Gate instead. This was among many setbacks that began to drag Owen's fortunes down.

Father Anthony Ravalli returned in 1866 to build a new mission church, using some salvaged parts of the original mission. The new building was closer to the fledgling community of Stevensville than to the stockade of Fort Owen. The mission included a blacksmith shop, and a pharmacy where Father Ravalli could practice his healing arts. Father Ravalli's interests in agriculture and engineering also led to more successful irrigated crops being grown locally. His success helped continue the shift of the valley's focus away from Fort Owen.

Nancy died in 1868, following which Owen suffered a decline into alcoholism that ultimately caused his commitment to an asylum in Helena. He died in the care of relatives back east in 1889, and his mill burned down the following year. His "fort," though, has been preserved as a historic landmark that, paired with St. Mary's mission, marks the starting point of the Bitterroot's modern history.

THE SALISH AND THE TREATY OF 1855

When the Salish chiefs arrived at Hell Gate Ronde to negotiate the Hellgate (or Council Grove) Treaty of 1855 they didn't have the loss of their ancestral lands as an item on their agenda. In addition to the Bitterroot Salish, the Pend d'Oreille and Kootenai nations met in the Missoula valley with territorial governor Isaac Stevens in July of 1855, expecting to negotiate some kind of end to their continual wars with the Blackfeet.

Instead, Stevens' agenda was the ceding of tribal lands to the U.S., and the creation of a reservation. The Pend d'Oreille, under Chief Alexander, and the Kootenai, led by Chief Michel, eventually agreed to the creation of the 1,280,000-acre Jocko reservation in the Mission Valley, centered on the St. Ignatius Mission.

The Bitterroot Salish, though, were reluctant even to speak of leaving their homeland, and their chief, Victor, held firm. Stevens agreed to a vague compromise: the Salish could remain in the Bitterroot Valley until the government completed a survey of both the Mission and Bitterroot valleys, and the President made a determination of where their reservation should be located.

Victor was also recognized thereafter as the head chief of the three confederated tribes. Chief Victor was a man caught, as much as any man could be, between two worlds. Known as Plenty of Horses until he was baptized Victor, he embraced the Catholic faith, but deflected the efforts of the missionaries to convert him into a farmer. He led hunting and war parties across the mountains to the land of

Victor, also known as Plenty of Horses, Principal Chief of the Bitterroot Salish until his death six years after this photo was taken in 1864. (BRVHS Photo)

the Blackfeet and Crow, but he also saw to it that no harm ever befell the whites moving into the Bitterroot at the hands of his people. As head chief, he frequently traveled to the Jocko reservation, but he never gave up the hope that his people would be allowed to remain in the Bitterroot Valley.

Upon his death on a hunting trip in 1870, Victor was succeeded as chief by his son, Charlot (or Charlo). In the interim, the valley had remained officially closed to settlement, but that technicality had been overlooked by the hundreds of white settlers who continued to establish homesteads in the area. Outnumbered roughly two-to-one by the estimated 600 Salish, they soon began clamoring for the Indians' removal to the Jocko reservation, insisting they needed protection as Indian wars with the Sioux and other "hostiles" heated up the prairie.

The Salish, though, took the opposite view, concluding that since the promised survey had never been undertaken and no determination made as to where they should live, the Great White Father must want them to remain in their beloved homeland.

In 1871 President Ulysses S. Grant issued an order declaring that the Bitterroot would, indeed, be surveyed and that the Salish should move to the Jocko reservation. Congress even extended the sum of $50,000 to the Indians to compensate them for their lands and homes. The Salish, though, sat tight, further agitating the whites in the valley. In 1872 Congress upped the ante and ordered their removal, opening the valley to legal homesteading by whites, and sending Representative James Garfield (later President) to negotiate the Indians' withdrawal. By including sub-chiefs Arlee and Adolph in the negotiations, and by promising the construction of buildings and the

Charlot, Victor's son, who was forced to lead his impoverished followers out of the Bitterroot Valley to the Flathead Reservation in 1891. Photo taken circa 1900. (BRVHS Photo)

payments of annuities, Garfield obtained the signatures and cooperation of the sub-chiefs – but not that of Charlot, whose signature was forged on the document.

Arlee and Adolph moved their followers to the reservation, and Arlee was subsequently recognized as head chief by the Department of the Interior. Most of the Salish, however, stayed put with Charlot, ignoring the provision that permitted them to receive 160-acre homesteads in exchange for dropping their tribal membership and becoming U.S. citizens. Instead, they subsisted poorly, living on the fringes of their ever-diminishing territory in poverty and neglect. Charlot had to live with accusations that he had sold his people out until the forgery of his signature was exposed in 1883.

The embittered Charlot refused to budge until the death of Arlee. Only then, in 1891, did he finally agree to lead his people out of the Bitterroot Valley, once and for all, to take up residence on the reservation north of Missoula. Gen. Carrington was sent from Fort Missoula to accompany the Salish on their march to the reservation, on October 15, 1891.

The sad parade of the Bitterroot Salish, as they moved north through the valley from their gathering point in Stevensville, on through Missoula, to the Jocko Reservation, must have been a heartbreaking sight to all but the most hardhearted settlers.

NEZ PERCE WAR OF 1877

The United States' campaign to eliminate or confine to reservations all the Indians of the West led to a telling episode in the Bitterroot valley in the summer of 1877.

Many of the Nez Perce tribe, who had once roamed the area where modern Idaho and Oregon join, were already willingly living on a substantial reservation when gold was discovered in the area. Settlers pressed the government to shrink the reservation, and, once again, many of the Nez Perce complied, moving onto the drastically reduced lands. Others, however, held out and remained outside the reservation, attempting to pursue their traditional lifestyle. In May of 1877 the government issued an ultimatum – move onto the reservation within 30 days, or face the consequences.

Roughly 800 Nez Perce, under the joint leadership of chiefs White Bird, Looking Glass and Joseph, held out. When three young men of their band murdered four white settlers, though, their hand was forced. After holding off a military attack at White Bird Canyon in Idaho, they decided to abandon their homeland and seek refuge with the Crow Indians of the Montana plains. They gathered all their possessions and moved, in a long column, across the Bitterroot mountains on the Lolo trail, pursued by troops under the command of General O. O. Howard, whom the Indians came to call "General Two-Day-Behind."

Hearing of the trouble coming their way, the citizens of Missoula erected a haphazard "fort" near the mouth of Lolo creek. Here, Captain Rawn of Fort Missoula headed a contingent of troops and volunteers. When the Nez Perce arrived, they tried first to parlay with the soldiers. When it became apparent they would not be allowed to pass on the trail, in the early hours of July 28, they simply detoured up the mountainside and around the fort, which quickly became known as "Fort Fizzle."

The Nez Perce entered the Bitterroot valley peaceably, inviting Chief Charlo of the Salish to join them. He reasonably declined, having problems enough of his own in the valley without joining forces with a band of "renegades."

"It was my father's boast that his hand had never in seventy years been bloodied with the white man's blood," Charlo declared, "and I am the son of my father. We could not fight against the Nez Perce because they helped me several years ago against my enemy the Blackfeet, but we will not fight with them against the whites."

Still, he gave them leave to pass through Salish lands and to pasture their horses on what was then still Salish ground, but warned them not to harm any whites. They camped for two days just west of Stevensville, in the area now known as "Indian Prairie."

Some of the volunteers who had "defended" Fort Fizzle were even permitted to pass unharmed through the Nez Perce camp on their way home. While the white settlers of the valley variously barricaded themselves inside other impromptu "forts" at Skalkaho, Corvallis (mockingly christened "Fort Skedaddle), and Fort Owen itself, the Nez Perce made their way south through the valley, trading for supplies with those who weren't in hiding. Stevensville merchants willingly accepted their cash in exchange for flour, coffee, sugar and tobacco, having been warned that if they refused to sell such items, the Indians "would take them anyway," according to merchant Henry Buck. The merchants weren't deterred from charging top dollar for the goods, though.

The Indians passed the hastily-erected forts in amusement, and made their way south, finally reaching the Big Hole on August 7. Believing their pursuers had given up, they didn't even send scouts back to watch for trouble, although some in the camp had visions of further conflict.

In the wake of their passage through the Bitterroot, many local men joined a hastily-summoned militia and marched with General Howard to the Big Hole where, at dawn on August 9, they attacked the sleeping Nez Perce camp. The Indians suffered the loss of many lodges which were burned, and 89 of their number died, including women, children, and elders. The Indians rallied and drove the troops out of their encampment, across a small creek, finally pinning down the troops on a mountainside, where they held them with sniper fire until the column of Indians could gather their remaining possessions and retire from the battlefield.

"Few of us will soon forget the wail of mingled grief, rage and horror which came from the camp four or five hundred yards from us when the Indians returned to it and recognized their slaughtered warriors, women and children. Above this wail of horror we could hear the passionate appeal of the leaders urging their followers to fight and the war whoops in answer which boded us no good," Gibbons wrote of the sorry battle.

Tom Sherrill, one of the Citizen Volunteers who took part in the Battle of the Big Hole. Many of the volunteers later regretted their participation, and felt the attack was unjustified. (BRVHS Photo)

The Nez Perce quickly loaded their few possessions on their horses, buried their dead as best they could, and abandoned the camp while their snipers kept the soldiers pinned down, all that afternoon and into the next day.

The unfortunate band made their way past Bannack, through the newly-declared Yellowstone National Park to the Crow lands, where their hoped-for alliance was once again denied. Determined, then, to join Sitting Bull in Canada, they made their way north across Montana, before being stopped almost within sight of the border. Colonel Nelson A. Miles intercepted them in the Bears Paw Mountains, and a six-day siege ensued, during which Chiefs Looking Glass and Ollukut died. Finally, on October 5, 1877, at the battle of the Bears Paw, Miles accepted the moving surrender of Chief Joseph, but not before a significant number had crept away to filter across the Canadian border with Chief White Bird.

The remainder were sent to a reservation in Oklahoma, where more died than had perished during their "war." Finally, Chief Joseph and his people were allowed to return to the Northwest, but not to their homeland. Joseph died on the Colville Indian Reservation in Washington in 1904.

Today, the site of Fort Fizzle along Lolo creek is commemorated with a historical marker, and the Big Hole Battlefield is a National Park Service site, with an interpretive center and informative programs.

THE COMMUNITIES OF THE BITTERROOT VALLEY

Captain John Mullan (who surveyed the Mullan Road from Walla Walla across Idaho and Montana to Fort Benton) established a military camp about ten miles south of Fort Owen in the winter of 1853, calling it Cantonment Stevens, after the governor of Washington Territory. Cantonment Stevens, which should not be confused with Stevensville, was soon abandoned.

A decade later, traders John Winslett and J.K. Houk arrived with a string of pack animals laden with trade goods. Owen, not needing the competition, probably shoo-ed them away, so instead they moved a mile south and parked them where Stevensville now stands. They put up a rude log building and commenced trading.

A year later, with other structures popping up around the new trading post, the settlers in the area got together to name their incipient town, deciding to follow Mullan's lead and honor the first governor of Washington Territory, Isaac Stevens. The newly-christened Stevensville consisted of two mercantile stores, a blacksmith

Stevensville's dilemma is as apparent as the cutoff road arrowing from the town out to the Wye on Highway 93. Unplanned strip development along the highway is siphoning business away from Stevensville's historic downtown. The scheduled four-laning of the highway has forced residents to begin confronting issues of land-use planning and the city's future.

shop and a saloon – pretty much the prototypical western watering hole. The date was May 12, 1864, and unknown to its namesake, Fort Owen's fortunes had just gone into decline.

Settlement of the area continued, in spite of the fact that by the terms of the treaty of 1855 the land south of Lolo creek was closed to whites. The Indians had no one to enforce their treaty rights, and they honored their pledge to do the whites no harm.

The gold strikes of 1862 that catapulted the communities of Bannack and Virginia City into being led to a bonanza of a different kind for the frontier community. Farmers found good soils and an agreeable climate in the valley, and a market hungry for their produce in the nearby gold camps.

Teamsters transported goods either north to Missoula and thence along the Mullan road, or south over what came to be known as Gibbons Pass into the Big Hole and on to Bannack.

Stevensville obtained a post office in 1868 and quickly grew to become the trading center of the Bitterroot valley. The Buck brothers began their family's long-running mercantile career in 1876, buying out Winslett and Houk's stake in the town. Statehood came in 1889, and four years later, when Ravalli County was carved out of the once-sprawling Missoula County, Stevensville was named the county seat. The town officially incorporated in 1899.

A view down the quiet Main Street of Corvallis, showing the schoolhouse that was built in 1915, and which burned in a spectacular fire in 1930. (BRVHS Photo)

Lee Metcalf

Stevensville's most famous native son is Lee Metcalf, who served in the U.S. House of Representatives from 1952 until his 1960 election to the U.S. Senate, where he served nearly three terms until his death in January of 1978.

Thoroughly Montanan (he was the first Montana native to serve in the Senate), Metcalf was born in Stevensville on January 28, 1911, and graduated from the University of Montana School of Law. Ambitious from the start, he served in the state legislature before moving up to assistant to the Montana Attorney General, then came a post as an Associate Justice of the Montana Supreme Court.

Metcalf's political leanings were decidedly liberal, but it is his legacy as a conservationist that earned him the honor of having a National Wildlife Refuge (just north of his hometown of Stevensville) named for him. Metcalf was a supporter of the landmark Wilderness Act of 1964, which created, among other areas, the magnificent Selway-Bitterroot Wilderness, and led the fight to protect other areas throughout the West. His office also played an important part in the Bitterroot clearcutting controversies that arose later in that decade, leading to radical changes in U.S. Forest Service harvesting policies. His tendency to decline publicity should not allow his accomplishments to be obscured.

Numerous other communities sprang up during this time. Many sputtered along

The Grantsdale General Merchandise store, built by Henry H. Grant in 1885, and many (or perhaps all?) of Grantsdale's proud male citizens. (BRVHS Photo)

The Bitter Root Development Company's sawmill was the cornerstone of Marcus Daly's planned new town of Hamilton. The dam backed up the Bitterroot river to form a mill pond for the sawmill's logs. (Montana Historical Society photo)

for a time before dying, but several have hung on to become viable communities that have lasted more than a hundred years.

At the northern extreme of the valley lies the community of Lolo, where a post office bearing the name Lolo Hot Springs was established in 1888. The name "Lolo" is of indeterminate origin – some say it's an Indian corruption of "Lewis," others claim it's the Salish rendering of an early trapper named Lawrence, but nobody is certain. What is known is that gradually the name stuck itself to everything around – the town, the creek, the valley, the peak, the pass. The historic (and somewhat more poetic) "Travelers' Rest," that Lewis and Clark affixed to their campsite and the creek, had largely disappeared from common usage until the recent upsurge of interest in the expedition

Florence, first called One Horse (for the creek on which it sits), was established by 1878. It was renamed in honor of Florence Hammond, the wife of Missoula businessman A.B. Hammond. Hammond was instrumental in bringing the railroad to the Bitterroot, mainly to serve his logging interests. Florence was a logging center, its boarding houses filled with lumberjacks and the air filled with the sounds of four sawmills running. In addition to creeks full of sawdust from the mills, early visitors found a bustling railroad depot, a greenhouse, a couple of saloons, and a cheese factory.

In 1881 the town of Garfield was platted near the center of the valley, hoping to take advantage of a likely Northern Pacific branch railroad line. The town was named in honor of the recently-assassinated president, James A. Garfield, who had also negotiated the removal of the Salish from the valley. Informed that the name

Darby celebrates a holiday with a parade, circa 1900. Note the A.C.M. (Anaconda Copper Mining) company store. (BRVHS Photo)

Garfield, Montana, was taken, residents agreed instead to name the town Victor, honoring instead the Salish chief who had lived on nearby Sweathouse creek. (Ironically, it had been Victor's son, Charlot, who had confounded Garfield by refusing to sign the treaty he proposed).

Victor grew quickly, spurred in part by the arrival of the railroad in 1887. In the 1890's it challenged Hamilton for the county seat, but couldn't counter Marcus Daly's influence. Hamilton won, and Victor's growth was blunted.

Corvallis grew out of a settlement on Willow creek, originally called Chaffinsville (or Chaffinville) and settled by the family of Elijah and Margaret Chaffin in 1864. A year later it was being pitched as "Willow Creek," but that name failed to take, too. A rough general store appeared in 1869, the year that a man named Herron proposed "Corvallis," a coined word taken from the French and presumed to mean "the heart of the valley." The name stuck, and the post office opened in 1870. The town was officially platted in 1879, but it has never incorporated.
Corvallis' fortunes have ebbed and flowed over the years, tied to the general state of agriculture in the valley. The apple orchards and sugar beet fields that once surrounded it are largely history, but the town has stubbornly refused to concede defeat, even after twice losing school buildings to fire.

West of Corvallis, nestled below Sheafman Creek, is the valley's youngest community. Pinesdale was settled in 1961 by a conservative sect of the Mormon church, led by Rulon C. Allred. His followers left Utah, looking for an area more tolerant of their beliefs, and bought the timbered townsite, a former ranch. The townsite is owned by the United Industries Corporation, which is controlled by the

A coal-burning steam locomotive of the Northern Pacific Railroad at a stop north of Corvallis, probably picking up empty apple crates. (BRVHS Photo)

church. Church elders effectively operate the town, although the town charter calls for governance by three selectmen and an advisory board, all directly elected by voters.

Pinesdale is a "closed" community of roughly 700 people, all church members. Among the distinguishing features of the sect is its tolerance of polygamy, and a strong desire for self-determination, one of the chief reasons they incorporated as a town in 1983. While visitors are cordially received, joining the community means agreeing to their unorthodox religious beliefs.

The town has evolved as a residential community, with most residents working at jobs outside the town. It supports a school, the Pines Academy, with students from kindergarten through sixth grade, and sends most children in higher grades to the Corvallis school district, which has benefitted from the added enrollment. City services are few, although Pinesdale does operated a sophisticated water supply.

Riverside was a promising town once known as Sanders Crossing, later

Hamilton's Central Meat Market at 307 W. Main, owned by jokester Percy Edwards (second from left). Note the clientele on the right. Circa 1910. (BRVHS Photo)

becoming River Siding, shortened to Riverside, when the railroad came through (Woodside derives similarly from Wood's Siding, named for the Rev. Wood). Riverside's fortune became linked to Marcus Daly, for its location provided the easiest access to his growing Bitter Root Stock Farm, and the sawmill located there provided much of the lumber for his ranch buildings.

Riverside soon discovered how fickle Mr. Daly's favor might be, when he platted the town of Hamilton just a couple miles up the tracks. Several business owners made the expedient decision to move to Hamilton, and loaded not just their belongings but their entire buildings on railroad flatcars and hauled them wholesale to Hamilton, or relocated them with teams of horses dragging them on sets of wagon wheels.

Riverside is marked today by a towering, never-used smokestack, built in 1917 to herald the arrival of a sugar-beet processing plant that was never completed. The Montana-Utah Sugar Co. was either a scam from the start, or it was defeated by sugar mill interests in Missoula that conspired to see that it failed. Either way, that one of

Another view of the "Big Mill," taken from the end of Desta Street looking northwest, circa 1900. (BRVHS Photo)

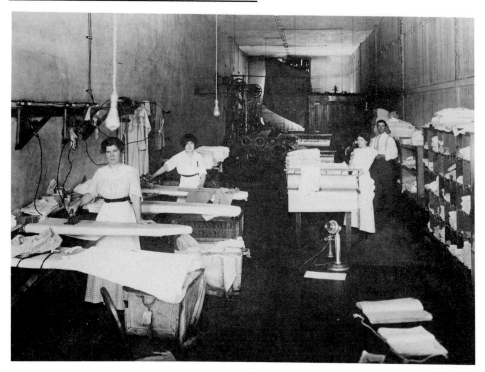

*Information on the photo sugg[...]
that this was taken shortly afte[...]
Hamilton was electrified, prol[...]
circa 1911, although the crate[...]
marked "Stevensville Steam."[...]
probably the Bitter Root Stea[...]
Laundry, which stood on the
northwest corner of Hwy. 93 [...]
Main in Hamilton. Either way[...]
hard to miss the enthusiasm o[...]
employees. (BRVHS Photo)*

*Harry Johnson operated the M[...]
Café in Hamilton, no doubt dr[...]
a distinguished clientele. (BRV[...]
Photo)*

the Bitterroot's most visible landmarks commemorates a failed business deal would surprise no one.

.   Grantsdale showed up on the map in 1885, founded by Henry H. Grant along Skalkaho creek at the end of the stagecoach road built south from Missoula. When the railroad was extended that far in 1888, the town boasted a hotel, drugstore, millinery shop, boarding houses and, shortly after, a newspaper, the *Bitter Root Bugle*.

Darby's citizens thought they had a say in naming their community, but they were wrong. They had voted in 1888 to call the town Harrison, in honor of the newly-elected President, but the Post Office informed them that a town of that name already existed in Montana. Postmaster James Darby took care of the problem by naming the post office for himself. Darby was "the end of the line" for the Northern Pacific's Bitterroot spur, which served a variety of sawmills over the years. Darby has also traditionally been the jumping-off point for travel to the East and West Forks of the Bitterroot River.

The town's heritage as a logging and sawmill town saw traumatic change in the 1980's and 90's. Depressed prices for forest commodities, decreased availability of cheap sawlogs, automation in the mills, protested timber sales, and other factors far beyond the control of Montana all conspired to crush the local logging industry. In a dramatic expression of frustration, a Darby sawmill organized "The Great Northwest Log Haul" in May of 1988. They needed logs to continue operating, and logs they got – over 300 loads delivered by trucks that started their run in Eureka, Montana, thundered down Highway 93, and pulled through the mill gates as news cameras rolled. Green "We Support the Timber Industry" signs appeared in nearly every business window, and "This family is supported by the Timber Industry" signs popped up on fenceposts along every road. Emotions ran high as everyone blamed everyone else for the industry's problems, but in the end the major mills closed, one by one.

While logging continues at a much-reduced rate, Darby's sawmills have closed and the forest products industry has come to focus on log homes, posts and poles, and chainsaw art. The strong identity that the town once drew from its lumberjack heritage is fading as it comes to embrace a tourism and recreation economy, quickly becoming the capital of the south valley's recreational paradise.

Many other communities have arisen in the valley, with various fates. Conner and Sula, astride the West Fork and East Fork of the Bitterroot river, respectively, have retained their post offices and a sense of community identity. Sula is named for Ursula "Sula" Thompson, the first white child born in the area.

Lone Rock and Carlton retain some sense of place centered around the school districts that bear their names, while Etna and Charlos Heights, once upstart communities, now retain neighborhood identities.

FROM TERRITORY TO COUNTY

When we speak of the Bitterroot today, we are largely speaking of the area now known as Ravalli County, although Lolo Creek and the community of Lolo should be included as well.

Claims to this land were disputed prior to the Lewis & Clark expedition. Although the concept of "ownership" might have seemed odd to them, the Salish occupied the valley until that time. The passage of the expedition solidified the United States' claim on the area, though, and in 1848, Congress declared it to be part of the huge Oregon Territory. Five years later, that was split, and this region became part of Washington Territory.

Washington Territory was split up into counties, and in December of 1860, Missoula County was established, with the county seat in Hell Gate (now Missoula). A further refinement of the boundaries in 1863 made the county part of Idaho Territory for a year, until Montana Territory was established in 1864. The first Territorial Legislature divided the state into nine counties, and reaffirmed the placement of the Missoula county seat in Hell Gate, an affront to those who supported the new community of Stevensville, with its heritage of St. Mary's Mission and Fort Owen.

At the time of statehood, in 1889, Montana had 16 counties, but in the next three decades those would divide and subdivide into the current 56. It was in the 1893 legislature that the creation of "Bitter Root County" was proposed by Edwin Smalley, a Stevensville representative, with a county seat (naturally) in Stevensville. In the course of its passage, the bill was amended to lop off the northern end of the county, leaving it in Missoula County, which coveted Lolo Pass, over which it was rumored a railroad line to Idaho would be built. The bill was further altered at the last minute to honor Father Anthony Ravalli, making it Ravalli County, and so it passed on Feb. 16, 1893. Stevensville's status as county seat was provisional, though, and soon to change.

THE COMING OF THE NORTHERN PACIFIC RAILROAD

Transportation through the Bitterroot was sketchy until 1867, when a road was finally surveyed from Missoula to the Skalkaho (later Grantsdale) area. Prior to that the trails established by the Salish were the primary routes into and out of the valley. The stagecoach road that the surveyors located was still no picnic–it forded the Bitterroot River twice, once north of Lolo to the west side of the river, then back to the east side near Bass Creek Hill. It continued south through Stevensville and Corvallis to a site on Skalkaho Creek, its southern terminus.

By 1883, though, valley residents were agitating for a railroad connection. Agriculture, logging and mining interests all saw access to markets as the prize, while settlers saw an end to the dusty, bumpy, and perilous (at high water) wagon or stagecoach ride to Missoula.

The Northern Pacific Railroad (NPRR) line was completed across Montana in September of 1883, with the final spike in the line linking the coasts driven near Gold Creek. Three years later the Missoula & Bitter Root Valley Railroad Co. was formed by local investors. The Northern Pacific could not legally build branch lines, but nothing could stop it from financing their construction and then buying them when completed, which is exactly what it did.

The location of the line was bitterly fought, with Stevensville and Corvallis arguing for an eastside route, but the financiers were invested in timber and mining, so on May 17, 1887, the line was begun, committed to a route that kept it on the west side, near the logging camps at Florence and Riverside, and the Curlew mine at Victor. Crews wrapped up the job on June 9, 1888, when the rails reached Grantsdale, and the line was officially dedicated. The branch was eventually transferred to the Northern Pacific as agreed.

Of course, this being the Bitterroot, residents soon came to feel that paradise with a railroad wasn't enough – they wanted a main line connection through the valley. Rumors twice circulated about new lines, one to be built over Lolo Pass, and another (even less likely) connection to Portland, but nothing ever came of either beyond the extension of track to Darby.

The railroad finally conceded the point to the eastside communities in the 1920's, when it relocated the mainline to take advantage of the sugar beet boom.

The use of railroads in logging the Bitterroot is an often–overlooked aspect of its history. Small, temporary lines would be built into the woods, the logs hauled out by hard-working steam engines, and the track torn up as soon as the operation was completed. Traces of these temporary lines can still be seen in some areas of the forest.

HAMILTON – Mr. DALY'S TOWN

Hamilton, which grew to become the largest city in the valley, was entirely the creation of Copper King Marcus Daly. Daly's copper mining and smelting interests

One of the last passenger trains in the Bitterroot steams past Lolo, bearing the Hellgate Elks Club of Missoula, on April 18, 1942. Run 2212, Elks Club Special, destination Hamilton, arrival time 5:30 p.m., one baggage car and three coaches. (BRVHS Photo)

in Butte and Anaconda made him one of the wealthiest and most powerful figures in Montana. The Irishman with a knack for mining first passed through the Bitterroot in 1864, on his way from Utah to the mining camps of Butte. At the time, he must have taken note of its good soils and abundant timber.

Daly made a fortune in Butte after purchasing the Anaconda mine in 1881. The Anaconda's silver vein played out quickly, but in its place Daly knew a rich body of copper lay. He enlisted the backing of his old friend George Hearst and built a smelter to reduce the ore. Around the smelter grew the town of Anaconda, and around the two grew the fortune of Marcus Daly.

After making his fortune, in the 1880's Daly turned to the Bitterroot valley for a summer home and a place to raise thoroughbred horses. He bought a home owned by Anthony Chaffin in 1886, then established the 22,000-acre Bitter Root Stock Farm

The Dalys' just-remodeled Bitter Root Stock Farm home, in a photo dated 1897. This house may have incorporated parts of an earlier farmhouse that stood on the site, and was itself swallowed by the neo-Georgian remodeling of the home that Mrs. Daly completed in 1910. (BRVHS Photo)

east of present-day Hamilton. The home he enlarged and remodeled in the Queen Anne style, then he set about proving his theory that the cool climate and relatively high altitude of the Bitterroot would produce the finest thoroughbred racing horses west of the Mississippi.

He also began buying logging interests in the area, to supply timbers for his mines in Butte. In 1888, Daly began purchasing sawmills operating in the Hamilton area. The widespread practice of staking mining claims, logging them off and then moving on to another claim led to a plentiful supply of cheap sawlogs.

Daly intended to capitalize on this, and hired James Hamilton and Robert O'Hara to survey, plat and establish a town. Hamilton was platted in September of 1890 (and officially incorporated in 1893). By 1891, the city of Hamilton was a going concern, quickly boasting a bank, a school, shops and hotels along its wide streets.

Marcus Daly: Irish immigrant, Copper King, founder of the Bitter Root Stock Farm, and father of Hamilton. (DMPT)

In one way or another, every street in the fledgling town bore Marcus Daly's imprint. Many, if not most, of the town's original businesses were controlled by Daly through his many holdings. Most of the men living in Hamilton worked for him, employed either by the Bitter Root Stock Farm, his sawmill, flour mill or other interests; they transacted their business at his bank, and bought their goods at the mercantile he operated. Guests in town stayed at his magnificent, three-story Ravalli Hotel, and found first-class entertainment at the Lucas Opera House. Several original Hamilton churches stand on land that he donated.

Sadly, most of these historic buildings have burned down, although the Banque Club occupies the building that first housed Daly's Ravalli County Bank.

The sawmill, completed in 1891, was located at the west end of Main Street, along the river. A dam backed up the river to form a mill pond, and in the spring during high water logs would be driven down the river all the way from the West Fork to Hamilton to feed the mill, which typically operated six to eight months out of the

Margaret Daly, wife of Marcus, with their daughter Margaret. (DMPT)

year, employing between 200–300 men.

Daly's brilliant mining instincts made his fortune, but political scheming was one of his favorite hobbies. He may best be remembered for his role in the "war of the Copper Kings," a titanic struggle between Daly and rival William A. Clark. The two locked horns over nearly every political issue in the 1880's and 90's, culminating in massive statewide voter fraud on both parts and a scandalous election in which Clark won a seat in the U.S. Senate, which then refused to seat him because of the gross and flagrant vote-buying.

Petty issues would serve as well as Senatorial elections, though. It is said that as Hamilton began to grow and succeed, Clark made an offer to buy the entire town of Grantsdale and to build a sawmill there to rival Daly's. He was rebuffed, the valley having been largely won over to Daly's side, and his payroll as well. (Another version of the story has Daly attempting to buy Grantsdale to save himself the trouble of having to build his own town).

Daly played a part in politics on a local scale as well. In an 1894 election, Corvallis sought to wrest the county seat away from Stevensville. Daly coveted the honor for Hamilton, but didn't have the political clout to swing it at the time, so he threw his considerable influence behind Stevensville's successful bid to retain it in that election. Immediately following the election he reversed course, and spent the next four years lobbying for another vote on behalf of Hamilton.

The 1898 contest went Daly's (and Hamilton's) way, but due to the bitter rivalry between the communities the county records had to be sneaked out of Stevensville at night on a prospector's pack burros.

Though the fortunes of all the communities in the valley have varied over the years, Hamilton has remained unchallenged as the economic and political center of the valley since its confirmation as the county seat.

THE BITTER ROOT STOCK FARM

The figure of Marcus Daly looms over the Bitterroot Valley like the mature cottonwoods that line the lanes he established. A poor Irish immigrant when he arrived, Daly was much-loved in his time as a champion of the "common man." But he was also known as a crafty man who liked to have things his way and who had the resources to see to it.

Likewise, the Bitter Root Stock Farm was established around Daly's passion for thoroughbred racing horses, and standard-bred trotters, which he hoped to prove would thrive in the Bitterroot valley. Although the farm also produced crops such as sugar beets and potatoes, horses were the focus of his efforts here, and the ranch was designed with horse breeding foremost in mind.

He succeeded wildly, producing horses that won numerous races back East. Of the 1,200 or so horses he owned, the most successful were Ogden, Hamburg, Prodigal, and Montana, and the best-loved of all, the celebrated Tammany, winner of New Jersey's Suburban Stakes in 1894. To celebrate that win, Daly erected a

The Daly Mansion is the elegant symbol of Marcus Daly's tenure in the valley. Founder of the Bitter Root Stock Farm in 1886, and the father of the city of Hamilton, Daly never lived to see the mansion in its present form. His widow Margaret accomplished the remodeling in 1910, and since then the mansion has had a fascinating history filled with Hungarian nobility and fine horses, public concerts and private parties. (Photo Barbara June)

sumptuous barn for Tammany, with cork floors and a velvet lining for Tammany's stall. "Tammany's Castle" still stands just east of Hamilton today.

That Daly doted on his horses is evidenced by the fact that he commissioned Henry Cross to paint large oil portraits of several of his favorites. He would also send oats from the Bitter Root Stock Farm on the train with the horses when they were shipped back East to race.

To facilitate the breeding and training of his racing stock, the ranch included barns capable of housing 600 horses, a dedicated veterinary facility, and four racetracks, two of them covered!

Daly built a summer residence on the Stock Farm from which to oversee his Bitterroot valley interests. The farmhouse converted into an elegant Victorian home served him until his death in 1900. Six years later his widow, Margaret, embarked on another extensive remodeling, hiring noted Missoula architect A.J. Gibson to design a magnificent new residence, incorporating parts of the original house but changing its appearance drastically.

Attorney Robert O'Hara, an agent of Marcus Daly's Bitter Root Development Corporation, became Hamilton's first mayor when the city was incorporated in 1894. (BRVHS)

In its place arose the Daly Mansion we see today, the largest private residence in Montana, a three-story, 24,000-square-foot, brick structure in the "Georgian Revival" style, completed in 1910. The home features 24 bedrooms, sharing fifteen bathrooms, with steam heat that is augmented by seven fireplaces, five of which feature Italian marble facing. Many rooms sport fanciful wallpaper imported from Europe, and the foyer is done in silk brocade. The Trophy Room was a 1914 addition.

The grounds are landscaped with a variety of non-native trees, most notably maples lining the entrance lanes that provide sensational color in the fall, and a giant, world-record prairie cottonwood. In addition to the main house, the grounds feature a greenhouse, laundry building, a playhouse for the kids, tennis court and a large pool, known as the "plunge," with dressing rooms.

The Daly influence in the valley continued long after Marcus' untimely death in 1900, from complications related to diabetes. The Bitter Root Stock Farm, though, suffered. His wife, Margaret, didn't share his passion for the horses, and they were sold in a grand auction at Madison Square Garden. With them went the groomsmen, stable hands, veterinarians, trainers and others associated with his racing operation. While the farm has continued to operate, it has never been on the scale of Daly's racing operation.

Margaret continued to spend time at the farm, and was generous toward Hamilton. She donated land and money for numerous projects, including the fairgrounds, the airport, the library, and the original Marcus Daly Memorial Hospital on Fourth Street, among many others. At her death, though, in 1941, the Daly Mansion was boarded up.

Daly's youngest daughter, Harriot (known as "Hattie") married Count Anton Sigray, of Hungary. The ranch ultimately passed into the hands of Countess Margit Sigray, their daughter, who married Baron George Bessenyey.

Margit Bessenyey, known to most simply as "the Countess," continued the tradition of raising horses on the Bitter Root Stock Farm, specializing (to no one's surprise) in Hungarian horses, her passion. For nearly 20 years the Countess sponsored the Bitterroot Competitive Trail Ride, an endurance event that drew horses and riders from throughout the country. It began as a two-day event, 40 miles the first day and 20 the second, but became a one-day, 60-mile event to provide a greater test of both horse and rider's endurance.

Upon her death the Bessenyey family elected to dispose of the mansion and its contents. Through their generosity, and the persistence of local citizens determined to preserve the building, the State of Montana acquired the Daly Mansion. A massive auction was held in 1986 at which the furnishings were sold, but some of the most important pieces were purchased by a consortium of local donors determined to keep the collection intact. Many others were ultimately donated back to the nonprofit Daly Mansion Preservation Trust, which now manages the building and grounds as a museum, offering tours and making the building available for special occasions.

The Bessenyey family continues to operate the Bitter Root Stock Farm primarily as a cattle operation, although a substantial portion of it was sold to the group that is developing a private golf and resort development, called The Stock Farm.

MINING AND THE BITTERROOT

The Bitterroot Valley has yielded much to the hands of those who have lived here, but has been stingy with its mineral wealth. Mining has been an iffy venture, although rumors of the big strike, just awaiting discovery, persist.

Father DeSmet is said to have been aware of various gold deposits in Montana, without ever divulging their location. Later, John Owen recorded the comings and goings of dozens of erstwhile prospectors, some of whom were actually in possession of rich findings, but most of whom were still looking.

In the late 1860's a productive vein of gold was discovered up Eight Mile Creek, east of Florence. A town briefly sprang up there fifteen years later, called Pyretees, but the ore played out by the turn of the century. Other small strikes turned up in the area, but never amounted to much.

In 1879 the Curlew mine was located, at the mouth of Big Creek, near Victor.

The Bitter Root Stock Farm pro
more than just racing horses. G
crops, cattle, pigs, sheep and a
herd were all part of the operat
Still, even the milk wagon shoul
drawn by a fine draft animal.
(BRVHS Photo)

A hundred years ago, just as no
hay was an important crop for a
horse operation. The just-visibl
building on the skyline with twi
cupolas was Daly's horse hospi
and veterinary operation. (BRV
Photo)

Ravalli County Fairgrounds were
nally located east of Hamilton's
oad depot, where the ballpark
stands. Marcus Daly raised
ing horses in addition to
oughbreds, and horse racing of
form or another remained a part
e Ravalli County Fair until the
0's. This photo is undated.
VHS Photo)

"Marcus," one of Daly's
thoroughbreds. Date unknown.
(BRVHS Photo)

The Hughes Creek mining camp teetered on the brink of becoming a town, but the diggings weren't quite rich enough to support it. (BRVHS Photo)

The Curlew, too, spawned a small community, called Curlew, and the railroad even ran a spur to the mine to haul the ore. Its heyday ran from 1891, when a concentrator was built on the site, until 1896, when the ore played out.

The Curlew saw renewed activity ten years after that, and again in the 1960's, but the grade of the ore and the price of gold never justified further development.

In 1893, the focus shifted to the West Fork, where placer deposits of gold were discovered in Hughes Creek. Those deposits were worked for some years, and this area remains the source of rich rumors regarding the "mother lode."

Mining claims were easy to stake, and a common scam in the valley was to file on a claim, log it off, then abandon it.

Other minerals have provided some mining activity in the valley. A mine near Darby for some years yielded fluorspar in commercial quantities, and another claim in the Skalkaho area produces vermiculite, but efforts to develop it commercially have repeatedly stalled.

BIRTH OF THE U.S. FOREST SERVICE AND THE BITTERROOT VALLEY

The Bitterroot National Forest dominates the valley. Much of what makes the

Bitterroot such a desirable place to live is related to the vast expanse of public land that lies at our doorstep. Its natural resources fuel our economy, while the scenic beauty it offers enriches our lives every day. Its mountain springs feed the streams that become the Bitterroot river, and the forests that cloak it provide habitat for the wild creatures that thrive there. And finally, the Selway-Bitterroot Wilderness Area offers a huge reservoir of largely-undisturbed forest for those who revel in remoteness or solitude, or who simply take comfort in its wildness.

For over a century the U.S. Forest Service has influenced the valley. The agency can trace its roots back to the Forest Reserve Act of 1891, and Congress established the Bitter Root Forest Reserves in February of 1897. Still, it remained for newly-hired Ranger Than Wilkerson and his partner H.C. Tuttle to erect the nation's first U.S. Forest Service ranger station at Alta, up the West Fork of the Bitterroot. They raised the flag over this historic building on July 4, 1899.

Wilkerson and his early Ranger counterparts were usually local men with good woodcraft and horse packing skills, but rarely did they have any formal training in forestry. In 1905 Elers Koch conducted the first formal Ranger and Supervisor tests, and they were strongly practical:

> The service wanted men who could ride and shoot and pack a horse and chop a log and run a compass line . . . the candidates had to show their ability in the field as well as write about it . . . the written test eliminated the illiterates, and the field tests insured that we got experienced hands.

The first rangers were kept plenty busy. The Bitter Root Forest Reserve existed on a map, but the boundaries had to be marked on the ground, a system of trails put in place and maintained, and the first timber sales to be administered. Among these other duties, they were also charged with helping to stem the epidemic of timber poaching taking place on public lands. The mere presence of a watchful ranger on the ground soon curbed the worst of that, and with that problem reasonably under control, they then turned their attention to the next serious cause of timber depletion: forest fires.

A September 1898, report by Richard Goode of the U.S. Geological Survey in *National Geographic* magazine on the state of the Bitter Root Forest Preserve delved into both problems:

> Practically, it has been impossible to place any restraint upon those desiring to use the timber on the public lands for any purpose whatever. One law provides that citizens may cut and remove for building, agricultural, mining, and other domestic purpose any trees growing on mineral lands, while another permits residents to take timber from non-mineral lands–and the land is usually held to be mineral or non-mineral as may suit the particular case..

> The most striking feature presented . . . is the large portion of it that has been burned over, nearly all of it having been visited at different times by fires and at least one-third of the standing timber having been destroyed . . . a scene of which all Americans should be ashamed. The aborigines held this region for many ages as a sacred trust transmitted from generation to generation. They recognized its beauty and utility and did naught to impair the grandeur of the one or the permanence of the other. And what has the Anglo-Saxon done? As a community is visited by a devastating scourge, as a face is disfigured by

some foul disease, so have the forests been visited and disfigured by him. Reaping where he has not sown and failing to restore where he has destroyed, a noble heritage is slipping away through carelessness and cupidity.

Such was the extent of the problem when the U.S. Forest Service was created.

The history of the Forest Service is tied closely to fire protection and Smokey Bear. For decades, crews of young men spent summers in the forest, fighting the seasonal fires that periodically threatened to consume huge swaths of timber.

Early lookouts would patrol from mountaintop to mountaintop, searching for smoke, and calling in fire reports on telephone wires strung for miles through the timbered wilderness. Later, lookout towers (more than two dozen on the Bitterroot National Forest at one time) replaced the tree-climbing smoke chasers, and later still aerial patrols fleshed-out the agency's arsenal of fire-spotting tools.

Events like the voracious Sleeping Child fire of 1961, that devoured several square miles of forest in a few hours, helped keep the public support for Smokey Bear's efforts strong.

Early logging focused on the Bitterroot's abundant stands of Ponderosa pine. This load was cut in the West Fork in 1893 for the Bitter Root Development Co. Early rangers had their hands full making sure that timber cut from the Forest Reserves was accounted for. (BRVHS Photo)

Some lookout towers were less than deluxe. The Ambrose Point lookout platform wasn't even the bottom of the line – in some cases lookouts had to shinny up a tree to scout the country. (USFS Photo)

Only in the last twenty years have forest managers come to understand that the ecosystem of the Northern Rockies is adapted to periodic fire, and that fire suppression may have had a serious detrimental effect on forest health, outraged reports in *National Geographic* notwithstanding.

While the public was once taught to see fire as a hugely destructive force raging through harvestable timber, the forest manager may now see periodic small-intensity fires as a powerful regenerative tool that can help recycle forest resources while actually reducing the threat of major conflagrations. The study of fire's role in the forest is still in its infancy, but the awesome rebound of life in Yellowstone National Park following the fires that raged in 1988 have helped reshape the public's perception of fire's role in the forest.

The major concern of fire managers on the Bitterroot N.F. now is the encroachment of homes and outbuildings on the forest fringe, where they are highly susceptible to fire. Landowners are learning to keep a cleared area around their homes, to prune low branches that could carry a fire into the crown, and to accommodate fire protection in their site plans.

"TICK FEVER" AND THE ROCKY MOUNTAIN LAB

The Bitterroot valley is no more susceptible to infestations of wood ticks than anywhere else in the Rockies. Come spring, as the snow goes off the ticks come out, and until the dry heat of summer banishes them they are a bloodsucking nuisance. Early in the 1900's, though, they were shown to be not just a nuisance, but the carriers of a life-threatening disease.

Rocky Mountain Spotted Fever was known before that time and, while rarely fatal, it was certainly a nasty infection. In the Bitterroot, though, a particularly virulent strain arose that was roughly 80% fatal among those who contracted it at that time.

The first symptoms of the disease were fairly general – fever, headache, joint pains, followed by a measles-like rash in the extremities, hence the moniker "Spotted Fever." Within two weeks, it could lead to death. How it was contracted and spread was a mystery, although "bad water" was suspected. Some even tied it to drinking snowmelt, a medical near-miss, as the ticks later shown to cause it were most active during the snowmelt season.

The first known fatality in the Bitterroot was a rancher living near Lost Horse Creek, in 1873. By the turn of the century, as more and more loggers entered the woods in tick-prone areas, the disease became more widespread.

Eventually, a pattern was discerned: the most serious cases arose on the west side of the valley, between Lolo and Darby. In 1901, valley residents had called on the governor for help fighting the disease. He responded by sending the Secretary of the State Board of Health, Dr. A.F. Longeway, and his colleague, Dr. Earle Strain, to the valley. They in turn enlisted Louis B. Wilson and W.M. Chowning, research pathologists from the University of Minnesota, to help.

After studying the distribution and course of the disease, these researchers

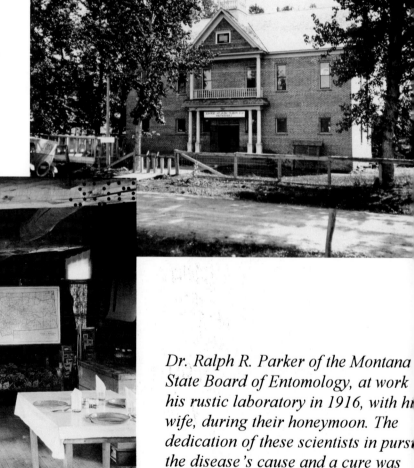

The Rocky Mountain Lab occupied the former Canyon Creek School, west of Hamilton, for ten years before moving to new quarters in Hamilton in 1928, when this photo was taken. Vaccine was produced in the older building for years. (BRVHS Photo)

Dr. Ralph R. Parker of the Montana State Board of Entomology, at work his rustic laboratory in 1916, with h wife, during their honeymoon. The dedication of these scientists in purs the disease's cause and a cure was nothing less than heroic. (BRVHS P

identified a malaria-like organism in the blood of victims, and concluded that it was probably tick-borne, but were unable to prove it. They were right about the ticks, but wrong about the cause. In 1906, the U.S. Public Health Service was summoned to investigate, and they dispatched Howard T. Ricketts. Working from Missoula, Ricketts was able to prove that the disease was caused by an organism related to but different from most bacteria, now known as "rickettsia."

He proposed a three-part solution: "dipping" livestock to kill ticks present on them, an eradication program for intermediate hosts, such as ground squirrels and other rodents, and the development of a vaccine.

Ricketts himself attempted to develop a serum, but his results were unsatisfactory. He died four years later after contracting typhus while working in Mexico.

Work on tick eradication progressed from a small log structure on Sweeney creek, south of Florence – tick central. Entomologists and researchers from several agencies worked from a crude cabin lab they christened Camp Venustus (after the scientific name for the wood tick, Dermacentor venustus).

They were joined by researchers from the U.S. Public Health Service once

The Rocky Mountain Lab was established by the State of Montana, but the operation was taken over by the U.S. Public Health Service. In response to citizen demands, the building featured a moat to prevent ticks from escaping, and a high fence to prevent children from entering. Circa 1928. (BRVHS Photo)

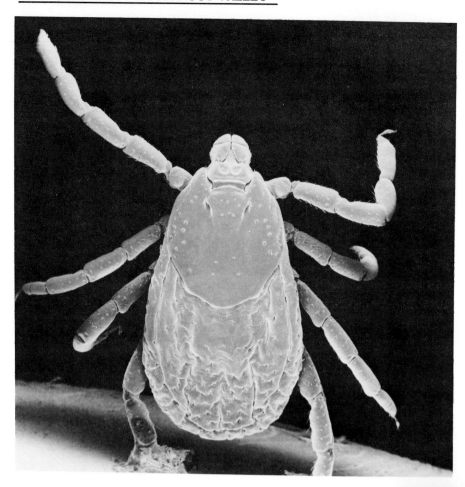

Public Enemy Number One: Dermacentor venustus, as the Rocky Mountain Wood Tick was known wh scientists began to pursue the cause Spotted Fever. (BRVHS Photo)

The end result of many years of research, during which several researchers lost their lives to Spotted Fever. The vaccine was regularly administered to schoolchildren in the valley until the 1960's, and was available to forest workers until treatment techniques proved reliable enough that fatalities from the disease became uncommon. (BRVHS Photo)

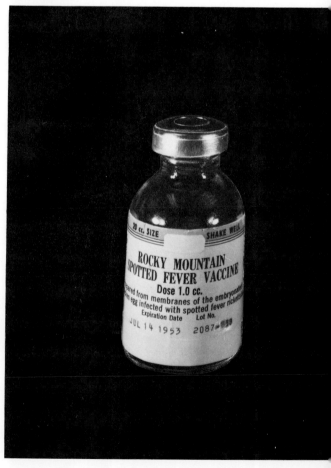

again in 1911, when they set up shop near Victor. Tick control became a hot issue, as ranchers resisted the orders to "dip" their prime stock in the arsenic-based solution that could cause skin irritations, and land speculators tried to quell talk of a virulent disease carried by bugs living on their high-dollar properties.

With funding from various sources, the researchers moved their lab to the recently-vacated Canyon Creek Schoolhouse west of Hamilton and it was there, through the combined efforts of doctors Ralph R. Parker and Roscoe R. Spencer, that they developed the first effective vaccine. Their work was so successful that others were drawn to work with them, and the state established the Rocky Mountain Lab in Hamilton.

The first building of what has grown to become the National Institute of Health's Rocky Mountain Lab was built in 1928, but not without some local opposition. The Bitterroot River was thought of as a barrier that blocked the ticks bearing the dangerous strain of Spotted Fever. Before angry residents would allow the research facility to be built on their side of the river, designers had to add a water-filled moat to the plans. This sufficiently placated the Hamilton residents, and the Rocky Mountain Lab (or RML as it is known) has since prospered. In 1931, the facility was taken over by the U.S. Public Health Service.

The RML produced a Spotted Fever vaccine first from infected tick tissue, and later from chicken eggs inoculated with the disease, and the serum was administered to schoolchildren every spring as the ticks emerged from their winter dormancy. Many Bitterroot old-timers still wince at the recollection of the injections, which could produce a painful reaction.

Over the years the Rocky Mountain Laboratory has grown from a single building to a large complex, recently renovated, where more than a hundred scientists and technicians from around the world now conduct cutting-edge health-related research. Their contributions over the years have helped conquer numerous insect-borne diseases, and today focus on both basic and applied research to halt the spread of communicable diseases.

One should pause, though, to remember the heroic efforts of those early researchers and their assistants, many of whom succumbed to Spotted Fever before they identified its cause and a vaccine was developed.

THE APPLE BOOM AND THE BIG DITCH

From the earliest days of Montana's white settlement the Bitterroot served as the state's garden spot, producing fruits and vegetables for the mining camps and, later, for Missoula's growing markets. St. Mary's Mission boasted the earliest apple orchards in the valley, and by 1896 county records showed more than 33,000 bushels of fruit being harvested annually from hundreds of acres of orchards. Growers felt the valley ideally suited to apple production. By the turn of the century, a group of men was ready to capitalize on that image in a big way.

Their plan, however, did not involve growing fruit or vegetables. Instead, theirs was a land promotion scheme of audacious vision.

The plan: acquire tens of thousands of acres of dry land, irrigate it with water from Lake Como via a canal 24 feet wide, six feet deep and 75 miles long, and plant it to apple orchards producing the famous Bitterroot MacIntosh apples. Then, sell those orchards to easterners who may never have heard of the fabulously productive Bitterroot valley, for many, many times what it originally cost.

The men who originated this plan included Samuel Dinsmore, who organized a ditch company around the turn of the last century. He had seen the success of Marcus Daly's Republican Ditch in delivering water to his Bitter Root Stock Farm, and in one of the rare instances of someone thinking bigger than Marcus Daly, promoted the idea of a ditch spanning the entire east side of the valley, irrigating thousands of acres of orchards. Among those who signed on were Frederick Nichols, an orchard promoter, R. W. Fisher of the Thousand Acre Orchard near Corvallis, W. O. Fish, manager of the Valley Mercantile, and Miles Romney Sr., who undertook the task of obtaining title to those thousands of acres where the Bitter Root Valley Irrigation Canal would run.

Such a gargantuan undertaking would need some serious financing, far more than could be obtained locally. The consortium turned to W. I. Moody, a Chicago financier who had previously spent time in the valley. Moody returned to the valley in the summer of 1905 to assess the project's prospects. He liked what he saw well enough to give the proposal the go-ahead, while he returned to Chicago to hunt up $3-4 million to make the project viable.

The elegant Daly Mansion awaits at the end of this maple-lined drive, but you wouldn't want to hurry in getting there. In some seasons, the mansion grounds are even more opulent than its extravagant interior.

Emboldened by Moody's confidence, the backers immediately set to work and raised the dam at Lake Como by 50 feet, dramatically increasing the water storage capacity of the impoundment. They then set to work building the "Big Ditch," as the canal system came to be known.

The ditch was laid out by surveyors to cross the Bitterroot River via a siphon under the river, which then emptied the flow into the head of the canal proper. The canal then took advantage of the valley's shallow gradient to cruise along the eastside foothills, where flumes and siphons kept it from intercepting all the streams draining the Sapphire range.

In order to scratch this 75-mile ditch out of the valley's hillsides, builders brought in a massive steam shovel. The shovel was mounted on railroad running gear, and as it progressed a short length of track was laid down ahead of it, and pulled up behind as it moved on. Crews erected trestles to ferry it across the many creeks and draws.

Thanks to Moody's efforts, in late 1906 the Assets Realization Company of Chicago signed on as the largest underwriter of the project and, with financing in place, construction efforts were redoubled. Excavation work directly employed nearly

Valley orchards still produce fruit for the local market. The Ravalli County Museum sponsors an "Apple Days" celebration in early October, where you can obtain fresh-pressed cider, apple pies, caramel apples, and hot apple butter prepared in a huge iron cauldron.

100 men, and indirectly boosted the valley's economy in numerous other ways. Teams of men fanned out to cut enough firewood to keep the shovel's boiler stoked, while others freighted supplies, provided clerical services, and even butchers prospered keeping everyone fed.

The project suffered one serious setback when a trestle bearing the shovel collapsed, dumping the machine unceremoniously in the bottom of the gulch. No workers were seriously injured, but the shovel had to be dismantled and muscled down the gulch to a makeshift landing where the pieces could be loaded on a logging wagon. The wagon was then drawn by dozens of resentful horses back up the steep path to the canal, where the shovel was reassembled, piece by piece, over nearly a month.

On another occasion a camp of workers was washed away by a flash flood that

By 1908, work on the ditch had progressed to the arid east side of the valley. Just visible in the photo is the water line running to the steam engine, keeping it continuously supplied with water–which is exactly what the ditch was to do for the east side orchards. (BRVHS Photo)

swept down Willoughby gulch following a violent storm in June of 1908. Three men lost their lives and numerous animals were swept away as well.

Meanwhile, the other pieces of the real estate scheme began to fall into place. Romney and others had secured extensive tracts of potential orchard land, paying between $2.50 and $15 an acre for most of it. It was platted and sold, largely in 10-acre tracts, which were advertised as capable of producing sufficient income from fruit crops to sustain a family in fine style. "$5,000 per year [income] and six months of vacation on 10 acres of orchard in the Bitter Root Valley," their ads screamed. Their intended market consisted of well-heeled Easterners who could afford a second home "out West," and their promotional brochures even offered to manage the land for five years on their behalf if they didn't want to get their hands dirty.

Of course, those tracts sold for a big profit . . . a *huge* profit . . . a whopping profit of between $400 and $1,000 per acre. And how were they sold? Skilled pitchmen traveled to exhibits at expositions back East to lure buyers to the Bitterroot with promises of an easy life as gentleman orchardists. Colorful brochures and advertisements pictured the valley as a pastoral Eden.

To support that myth, the developers platted the dream town of Bitter Root,

The "Little Giant" was one of six steam shovels employed in digging the miles of canal that became the Big Ditch. (BRVHS)

north of Stevensville in the Three Mile neighborhood. They hired an upstart Midwestern architect named Frank Lloyd Wright to design the flagship Bitter Root Inn, which was completed in 1910, and included its own water system and electrical power plant. By comparison, Stevensville wasn't electrified until the following year.

Wright also designed the development at University Heights, near Lake Como. This project included a central clubhouse with a dozen rustic cabins, designed to attract a crowd of well-off university professors who might enjoy summering in the Bitterroot on their own orchard properties. Crews completed this project in 1910.

(Wright is reputed to have designed several other buildings in the Bitterroot as well, although conclusive proof is lacking.)

Arriving in Missoula by train, potential buyers were met at the station by promoters driving large red (the color of MacIntosh apples) Locomobiles, still a novelty at that time, and whisked off to the brand-new Bitterroot Inn. There they received the royal treatment, including free drinks and access to a golf course, until they signed a contract to purchase their orchard tract.

Meanwhile, crews worked feverishly to plant orchards all over the east side, and in spite of the fact that the ditch hadn't yet begun delivering water, many began to flourish. Successful orchards already dotted the west side, and now the entire

Even while the ditch was being completed, potential orchard-buyers (typically midwesterners) were wheeled about the Bitterroot to view orchard tracts for sale. (BRVHS Photo)

valley seemed poised to offer a life of bounty to all.

Work on Como dam and the ditch peaked in 1909, by which time a dam had been raised 50 feet, quadrupling the surface area of Lake Como, and enabling irrigators to store enough water to see them through a typically dry Bitterroot summer. The first water was turned into the ditch in that year.

For a time it seemed like it all might just work. Some orchardists built homes on their new tracts and tended their quickly-maturing trees, while others allowed the promoters to look after their holdings, which they did with some success for several years.

Of course, stories like this never have a happy ending. Cash flow problems

e University Heights Club House was focal point of the Lake Como orchard velopment. Investors were encouraged build homes nearby, and take their als at the Club House. Note the fine nt at the bottom, offering two dresses for the Como Orchard Land .: one in Darby, the other in Chicago. RVHS Photo)

The Frank Lloyd Wright-designed Bitter Root Inn was to be the focal point of a planned community in the Three Mile area, north of Stevensville. Starting in 1909, potential buyers were housed here, and given the royal treatment – until their contract was signed. The building burned in 1924. (BRVHS Photo)

Displays of Bitterroot Valley produce were sent east to various expositions to attract investors. This attractive display features a model of the Charlos Heights clubhouse, as well as model cars and houses. (BRVHS Photo)

caused the Big Ditch Company to founder in 1918, and the Chicago investors who held the notes on the company foreclosed on them, but ended up losing nearly $4.5 million themselves. A reorganized company in turn failed, and the farmers themselves took over the project as the Bitter Root Irrigation District in 1920.

The weather, too, which had smiled on the orchardists for an unusually long time, turned nasty, and several years of early frosts were followed by several years of drought, decimating harvests and driving investors off their plots in droves.

When the lovely Bitter Root Inn burned to the ground in 1924, it was simply the final chapter in a story with a predictable ending. The Bitterroot, with its highly variable soils and its capricious weather was never destined to be anyone's agricultural paradise.

Today, the Big Ditch still operates, and the vision of its creators lives in the green hayfields of the east side, though to a much smaller extent than they hoped. Fortunes were made and lost over the Big Ditch and the Apple Boom, but the enduring legacy is the network of irrigation ditches that continue to feed thirsty crops

The MacIntosh apple was favored by most growers. It certainly seems to suit these two girls. (BRVHS Photo)

While apples are no longer the focus of Bitterroot agriculture, they're still part of the picture, and apple cider is still produced locally in the fall, just as it has been for a century. (BRVHS Photo)

– and to nourish the continual hopes of next year's bonanza.

One other lasting legacy of the Apple Boom is the Western Agricultural Research Center, east of Corvallis. This is a research station established by the legislature in 1907 and administered by Montana State University, with the original mission of aiding apple growers in the valley. They planted experimental orchards and evaluated which varieties grew best, given the valley's soils and climate, but their mission has broadened as the focus on apples has diminished. A dozen researchers now work on the station's 30 acres, which they use to study biological methods of weed control, orchard crops, and alternative crops suited to the valley, including medicinal herbs.

THE "BITTERROOT CONTROVERSY" AND THE U.S. FOREST SERVICE

Few things have had a more profound influence on the Bitterroot Valley in the last 100 years than the U.S. Forest Service and the management of the Bitterroot National Forest.

For instance, it was a 1908 Executive Order that changed the official spelling to make Bitter Root a single word, at least as far as the National Forest was concerned. That's a battle still being fought, with "Bitter Root" prevailing among those who wish to conserve the name's historic origins, but "Bitterroot" winning out in modern usage.

However you spell the name, though, the "Bitterroot Controversy" that raged from the mid-60's through the early 70's can clearly be counted as one of the most important legacies of the Bitterroot valley on a national level, causing major changes in forest policy nationwide.

The Bitterroot Controversy arose because the concept of "Multiple Use" of forest lands seemed to catch on more quickly with the public than it did within the production-oriented Forest Service of the 1950's and 60's. Large segments of the public began to recognize that the frantic rate of logging in those years threatened not just forest esthetics, but potentially wildlife and clear water as well as other values.

The origins of the controversy are obvious, in hindsight. Following World War II, a postwar housing boom focused pressure on the Forest Service to provide ever more timber for construction. This pressure resulted in dramatically increased logging on the 1.6-million-acre Bitterroot National Forest over the next quarter century.

Logging scars on the mountains had been a part of life in the valley since the 1880's. Marcus Daly built Hamilton around his logging efforts, and photos of the valley from that era confirm that the mountains were cleared of the valuable yellow pine (Ponderosa) halfway to their summits. By the 1950's, though, much of the easily-harvested pine was gone, and to feed the nation's appetite for lumber, harvesting was moving on to other species, including Douglas-fir, lodgepole pine and spruce, and to increasingly remote and environmentally sensitive sites.

The Forest Service based its harvesting plans on a number of factors, but was

The policy of "clearcut, terrace, and plant" was a version of industrial forestry that very nearly led Bitterroot conservationists to riot. While some foresters continue to argue that the forests were not grossly overcut in the 1960's, most will agree that the terracing contributed to excessive siltation, and was a visual nightmare. (USDA Forest Service)

guided primarily by the principle of "sustained yield." This implied that in any given year, the allowable cut should not exceed a figure that could be sustained indefinitely. In 1956, the Forest Service announced that its policy was to log right up to the "allowable cut" figure.

That "allowable cut" on the Bitterroot National Forest took a number of alarming (and to some, suspicious) leaps over the next ten years, rising from 12.5 million board feet in 1957 to 63 million board feet in 1966. "Getting out the cut" required a rat's nest of roads (engineering plans called for up to six miles of road per square mile), and the extensive use of clearcuts on terrain not always well-suited to such a scalping.

Clearcuts

Clearcutting is a method of timber harvest in which every woody stem within a given area is cut. The trees large enough to be sawn into lumber are hauled to the mill, and the remaining material is piled and burned.

Clearcutting is a reasonable harvesting method on appropriate terrain and

Supplying backcountry operations required packers with sophisticated skills, and reliable pack stock. The USFS contracted with some packers, but maintained their own stock and experienced employees as well. (BRVHS Photo)

to achieve specific results. Its classic application is to control mistletoe infestations, but it is also the method of choice to convert a stand of uneven-aged trees to a uniform, even-aged, same-species stand.

The resulting lack of natural regeneration, the lack of shade for seedlings, and the potential for erosion with such a level of disturbance makes it unsuitable in many areas. Further, it is a highly visible form of logging, and when applied in large blocks it is particularly unsightly.

In addition, the Bitterroot National Forest began experimenting with "terracing" mountainsides in 1964. While bulldozing terraces may very well be a highly-effective way to grow trees on steep mountainsides, the use of heavy equipment on unstable mountain soils sped loads of sediment into the streams, and altered the natural snowpack runoff. More important, however, it was highly visible and really, REALLY, ugly.

The program of "clearcut, terrace and plant" was a brilliant way to manage a forest in which feeding the local sawmills was the singular objective. It was also a certain recipe for inciting conservation-minded locals to riot, which happened shortly.

Logging remains a contributor to the valley's economy, even though at present no sawmills remain in the valley. Both Forest Service and private timberlands contribute raw materials, and the log home industry and a few local post-and-pole outfits represent the manufacturing side of the industry.

What lit the fuse was a controversy over the Magruder Corridor, the tract of land flanking an existing road that extended along the southern boundary of the Selway-Bitterroot Wilderness. When Congress passed the Wilderness Act of 1964, the Selway-Bitterroot was one of the "instant Wilderness Areas" it created, but the management of the Magruder Corridor was left unresolved. When the Forest Service suggested that it might be opened to logging or other development, a "Save the Selway" group sprang up in the Bitterroot, led by the respected forester Guy Brandborg, who had recently retired from the Forest Service as Supervisor of the Bitterroot National Forest.

The Forest Service foolishly dug in its heels over the issue, spurring strong local opposition and cementing alliances among conservation groups. An independent panel, appointed by the Secretary of Agriculture, concluded that the area should be managed for the benefit of fisheries and watershed, historic values, and recreation, a victory for the conservationists.

A growing number of people, meanwhile, were looking around at the ever-multiplying clearcuts, and realizing that this was something potentially unhealthy. When Brandborg, with considerable credibility, added his voice to those who claimed the allowable cut was too high and that the clearcuts were harmful, even some local loggers began to question the situation. The now well-organized conservation groups began to pelt the Montana congressional delegation with letters and requests to call the Forest Service logging off. In typical Bitterroot fashion, other groups representing the timber industry quickly formed and began their own campaigns in defense of the cutting.

The debates that ensued culminated in a series of highly-critical articles in the *Missoulian*, and ultimately in Congressional hearings. In May of 1970 the Forest Service produced a report acknowledging some mistakes, but it was upstaged in November of that year by the report of a select committee headed by Arnold Bolle, Dean of the School of Forestry at the University of Montana, and handed directly to Senator Lee Metcalf.

The effects of the "Bolle Report" on Forest Service policy nationwide would be difficult to overstate. For the first time, a group of forestry professionals had broken ranks to slam the Forest Service for their practices. Many in the Forest Service argued that the report was based on an agenda for change that had little to do with the facts of the controversy, but the Bolle Report had a momentum all its own, which led to further congressional hearings, chaired by Idaho Senator Frank Church, in 1971.

The Forest Service quickly went into defensive mode, acknowledging the mistakes it had made, and promising to back off on the clearcuts, reduce the miles of road to be built, and to work with landscape architects to design cutting units with less visual impact.

The Forest Service also began to acknowledge that the management of public lands involved a good deal more than selling sawlogs, and that public involvement in their decision-making was critical. (It's a lesson they are still learning, as contentious watchdog groups such as the Friends of the Bitterroot continue filing appeals of their actions to this day, even though harvesting has been reduced to an average of under 10 million board feet annually).

The debates that raged over clearcutting on the Bitterroot National Forest affected forest policy nationwide, and the forest was deluged with visitors who wanted to see the ground in question. According to Forest Service veterans, at one time in the early 70's so many "show-me" trips were scheduled to show both foresters and environmentalists around that they had to coordinate their schedules in the morning to avoid running into each other on the narrow logging roads.

That controversy, while not entirely settled, has since evolved into many of the environmental battles that have erupted and which continue to involve the Bitterroot National Forest. Some of those issues include:

•Wolf and grizzly reintroduction. Wolves are now present in the area, but the re-introduction of grizzlies is opposed both by those who fear the bears, and by those who fear that their access to the forest will be limited in order to protect the bear. Proponents of re-introduction are themselves split over how much area they need, and the level of protection they should be accorded.

•Wilderness dams. The Bitterroot National Forest contains more wilderness dams on high lakes than any other forest. Many of these dams, built to provide late-season water for irrigation, date back to the 19th century, and are beginning to show their age. The issue of how maintenance should be carried out on existing structures "grandfathered" into a statutory Wilderness Area is a difficult and potentially costly one. Wilderness purists would like to permit hand-tools only, although they have acceded to the use of motorized equipment in some locations. Dam owners and operators would like to be able to use heavy equipment to make repairs quickly and efficiently.

•Fire suppression. The Bitterroot National Forest first experimented with a "let-burn" policy within the Wilderness in 1972, when a lightning-caused fire was allowed to burn for three days, consuming an area the size of a comfortable living room. Since then, the program has expanded not only to allow some galloping wilderness wildfires, but even to ignite fires in areas where fuels have accumulated to dangerous levels. Issues of air quality and hazards to life and property make this a delicate proposition, but restoring fire to its historical role in the forest is an important ecological concern.

•Logging practices. Clearcutting continues on the forest, although on a much smaller scale, but even salvage sales following wildfires come under close scrutiny to determine their effects on watershed protection, wildlife, and forest esthetics. Forest road-building practices are all also an area of contention in which Forest Service officials and concerned groups of local citizens continue to seek accommodation.

Selway-Bitterroot Wilderness

As many of these issues were coming to a head and timber production on the Bitterroot National Forest was escalating, Congress took action to balance things somewhat by passing the Wilderness Act in 1964. Overnight, the 1.3 million acres of the Selway-Bitterroot Wilderness received the highest level of protection our country can afford. Wilderness designation is reserved for areas that offer outstanding opportunities for solitude, and which remain largely untrammeled by man – and the Selway-Bitterroot is an outstanding example.

The wilderness area is accessed by a network of trails that lead to many, but

by no means all, of its lakes and peaks. It offers abundant fish and wildlife, tremendous vistas of mountain scenery, magnificent, untouched forests, and year-round recreational opportunities, but by far its most valuable attribute is simply its wildness. It remains an area apart, where man is no more than a visitor, and that is a resource beyond value.

Areas of the wilderness register off the scale of a chart devised to measure recreation area attributes. Blodgett Canyon offers a perfect introduction to the area's charms, but the further you can hike and the longer you can stay the better will be your appreciation of this magnificent stretch of country.

In the last analysis, wilderness is special because it is land set aside for its own sake, not for ours. While the Selway-Bitterroot Wilderness offers such human-oriented amenities as spectacular sights, clear water, challenging big-game hunting and fishing, and recreation opportunities for every season, it is our absence that defines it as a wilderness, and visitors should keep in mind that they should leave no trace of their passing.

Currently, the Bitterroot National Forest is broken up into three ranger districts, headquartered at Stevensville, Darby, and the West Fork/ Sula, with the forest Supervisor's office in Hamilton. The BNF oversees most of the forested land in the county, both in the Bitterroot range and in the Sapphires.

The Forest Service adheres to the "Multiple Use" concept, attempting to ensure that the public lands will accommodate recreation users, wildlife, grazing rights, and watershed protection as well as timber production.

While the offering of timber sales continues to provide employment for area loggers, log home manufacturers and others in the timber industry, the Bitterroot National Forest is probably most familiar to valley residents and visitors as a recreation site. The Forest manages eighteen developed campgrounds, and more than 1,600 miles of trails beckon to hikers and equestrians, although not all of those trails are maintained. Forest roads offer access to hikers, berry pickers, fishermen, and hunters and, in winter, some are open to snowmobilers as well.

THE TRAPPER CREEK JOB CORPS CENTER

One of the brightest successes in the Bitterroot has been the Trapper Creek Job Corps Center, located up the West Fork. Its roots go back to the Depression, when work centers were established around the country and jobs with the Civilian Conservation Corps were the only jobs to be had in many areas. The CCC worked with the Bitterroot National Forest on fire suppression, road and trail construction, tree planting, and more, and one of the work camps was located up the West Fork.

When Congress created the Job Corps in 1965, under the Office of Economic Opportunity, it was logical to use existing sites. Since that time, the Trapper Creek Job Corps has grown to accommodate more than 200 young enrollees at a time, learning various skilled trades ranging from carpentry and concrete masonry to

winter it's an avalanche-prone shelf where you might not want to linger – but in ~mer, it's the world's finest campsite. The alpine lakes of the Bitterroot offer some ~e country's most spectacular backpacking destinations, and the fishing isn't bad, ~er. . .(Dale Burk photo)

culinary arts. A co-ed facility now managed by the Department of Labor, the Trapper Creek center boasts one of the higher job placement rates for such facilities nationwide. Enrollees may also be pressed into service for fire suppression.

Job Corps students have contributed to many Bitterroot projects, working on the Fairgrounds facilities and fashioning benches for Hamilton parks, as well as other public works projects. Still, for such a large institution, it has a fairly low profile; the most contact most valley residents have with enrollees is either going to a movie the same night as a busload of enrollees, or seeing them marching proudly in the Ravalli County Fair parade.

Overturf Excursions operated the "Admiral Dewey," a stern-wheel steamer on Lake Como, circa 1900 – a sedate, sociable contrast to the modern jet ski. (BRVHS Photo)

PART THREE: RECREATION

THE BITTERROOT RIVER

Over the years, gold prospectors found a handful of small, paying claims in the Bitterroot mountains – the Curlew mine, Hughes Creek and the Eight Mile district – but they never recognized the vein of pure silver that issues from the granite of those mountains: the Bitterroot River.

The river has enriched more lives than gold ever will, and the resource is nearly infinite, if it is protected.

First among its gifts, it offers the simple aesthetic purity of moving water. Its channel meanders through a wide valley, with panoramic views of dramatic, snow-capped mountains. Its clear, cold water offers a variety of recreational pleasures, but the simplest and most accessible remains the happy experience of sitting on its banks and watching it burble along.

Many, though, cannot sit for long with such water at their feet. The river invites rafting, canoeing, kayaking, inner tubing and swimming – on a warm summer's day. With water temperatures that typically reflect its icy origins, even in August it may not invite swimmers to linger too long.

Over the years the Bitterroot River has been given many names. The Salish may have known it variously as the Red Willow (Ootlashoot) or literally as the Spitlem Seukn, for "waters of the bitter root." Meriwether Lewis elected to call it Clark's River, one of the few features they named for themselves. Early trappers referred to it as Courtine's Fork of the Flathead, while later trappers (including Alexander Ross) first called it the Bitter Root. When Father DeSmet erected St. Mary's Mission, he christened the river after it, and maps drawn by the Jesuits refer to it as St. Mary's River. Some may have called it the Missoula River, but that never apparently came into wide use. When Forest Service mapmakers put it on paper as the Bitterroot River, it finally stuck.

The river is navigable from its source, the confluence of the east and west forks near Conner. Above that, much depends on the time of year, the water level, and one's willingness to scrape the bottom of the boat. Both forks lend themselves to floating in rafts, pontoon boats, kayaks, and even canoes after the initial high water has subsided in early summer, although drift boats are better left on the main river stem. As summer progresses, water levels drop and the East Fork becomes much better for wading than for floating. The West Fork will still float a raft, due to releases from Painted Rocks reservoir, but late in the season it may involve some judicious portages over shallow passages. Scouting for log jams is a good idea in any season.

The main river stem, however, normally bears enough water to float just about any reasonable watercraft, although such hazards as log jams and "sweepers" remain, lurking around bends waiting to snare unwary floaters. The water is particularly swift only during the runoff season, and "rapids" hardly exist at all, but the river periodically claims victims who disregard its still-considerable power and perils.

FISHING

The star attraction of the river, of course, is the Bitterroot's wild trout fishery. Years ago, Montana's Department of Fish, Wildlife and Parks moved away from the concept of stocking streams with hatchery fish to be caught and consumed, to a policy of encouraging the health of the wild trout fisheries in the river.

The Bitterroot is a highly productive river. Trout thrive throughout most of its length: rainbow, brown, cutthroat, and bull trout inhabit its waters, with brook trout teeming in the streams that feed it. Whitefish angling remains popular in winter, and illegally introduced pike, unfortunately, have been caught in the lower, warmer reaches below Stevensville.

The river remains almost irresistible to anglers, year-round. Whitefish anglers may be seen standing on ice shelves in January, flinging hypothermic maggots to their fate; not far from them in their zeal are those who fish the so-called skwala hatch in March and April, when the first relatively warm days bring on the season's first stonefly hatch. It provides for some dramatic fishing – in some very cold water.

A mountain stream cascading down-canyon pauses to gather itself. Did you pack your fishing gear?

The fishing gets poor during high water, usually in May or June as the snowpack melts off. The river becomes cloudy with sediment and runs dangerously high, and the streams likewise swell with snowmelt. Anglers bide their time until late June or early July, when the river and streams drop back to manageable levels and the fishing season surges to its peak.

Fishing regulations change from year to year; anglers should pick up a current set of regulations from any of the sporting goods shops in the valley. Sections of the river are typically catch-and-release-only year-round. Other segments may have possession limits by species, and whitefish angling may be open year-round.

Some stretches are limited to artificial lures only, but no matter where you fish, you can expect some disdainful, or even downright hostile glances if you show up with a can of worms and leave with a (legal) stringer of fish. The catch-and-release, fly-fishing cognoscenti have long labored to develop a low-impact ethos on the Bitterroot.

The river drops by late summer as the snowpack is depleted, but irrigation diversions also take a heavy toll on the streamflow. Trout Unlimited and other organizations have now reserved water in Painted Rocks Reservoir to be released in August to maintain streamflow in the river, and this has been very effective at preventing the nearly bone-dry stretches of the river that formerly characterized late

What could be more relaxing than a day on the river? Fishing isn't just a pastime on the Bitterroot River, ranking somewhere between a religion and an industry.

summer. Still, this remains perhaps the hardest time of year for the fishery, as flows drop and the temperature climbs.

By September and October, though, the flows are restored somewhat as irrigation water is diverted back to the river – and the trout get hungry again, preparing for winter. This is a time of some spectacular fishing on crisp, autumn days, on an uncrowded river. Don't tell.

Those unfamiliar with the river would do well to consult with any of the numerous local fly-fishing shops or river guides for advice on fishing or floating the river. Be prepared, however, for vague, general answers, as they may not be inclined to give away trade secrets to non-paying customers.

Fishing the mountain streams and high lakes is mostly a summer/fall proposition, as the streams tend to be swollen in spring...and the lakes may be frozen into early summer. But when the streams drop and clear following high water, they provide wondrous opportunities to catch pan-sized fish in pristine mountain streams, an experience that is hard to beat. Nearly every major tributary to the Bitterroot can be accessed by a trail – or, in some cases, a road – following it to its source.

The high mountain lakes may remain frozen and snowbound until June or July, but when they open up, are those fish hungry! Because of the harsh conditions under which they live, few of the fish in those alpine lakes ever grow to much of a size, but the pleasure of fishing for them in those high, rocky basins is reward enough. Some of the alpine lakes are barren, so it's best to check with a reliable source before setting off on a grueling hike to a high lake.

Lake Como and Painted Rocks Reservoir offer the only significant lake fishing in the valley. Both are drawn down dramatically for irrigation purposes by late summer, but still offer reasonable fishing for planted, hatchery fish.

HIKING

Entire books have been written about the hiking opportunities in the Bitterroot. It doesn't take much imagination to grasp the bounty with which a hiker is presented in the Bitterroot.

It's not a bad idea to pick up a hiker's guide at a book store or sporting goods store, just for the wealth of trail information and clear directions to trailheads. It's also nice to have a systematic way to check off those trails as you walk them!

Every canyon in the Bitterroot Mountains has a trail, it seems, enticing the dedicated hiker to try them all. The Sapphires offer fewer trails, largely unprotected by wilderness designation, that still offer satisfying forays into remote mountains.

Often overlooked, due to the popularity of the Selway-Bitterroot, is the Anaconda-Pintler Wilderness, accessed from the East Fork of the Bitterroot. Hiking here also offers a remote, pristine, wilderness experience in high mountain country dotted with lakes and streams.

Check with the appropriate Forest Service Ranger District for regulations on use of the Wilderness. Limits to the number of people in the party, requirements for

rs may be rewarded by scenic surprises at every turn in the trail. This natural three miles up Blodgett Canyon is one of very few such features to occur in a ite formation, rather than sandstone. (R. Lawrence photo)

weed-seed-free feed for pack stock, and bans on campfires vary from area to area, and are important tools for maintaining the wilderness.

Backpackers will exhaust themselves trying to explore every corner of the country. Many of the westside canyons harbor a high, alpine lake, frequently 10-12 miles up the canyon near the crest of the range. That's a long hike, going uphill, but a three-day trip makes it much more reasonable. Trails join some of the canyons, making it possible to do a loop hike, but in most cases it involves some overland bushwacking to complete the canyon-to-canyon segment. This is recommended for serious, experienced backpackers only, as the terrain gets challenging.

Many tempting low-elevation day-hikes beckon as well. Both the Teller Wildlife Refuge and the Lee Metcalf National Wildlife Refuge offer short hikes on the valley floor, and the City of Hamilton owns a good deal of wetland along the Bitterroot River that is open to the public as well, offering a pretty reasonable opportunity to sit in solitude in a remote-feeling location to watch the river go by.

A well-maintained trail also encircles Lake Como, providing a longer loop, with the spectacular cascades at the lake's inlet as a bonus. This very accessible trail offers a great introduction to hiking in the Bitterroot for youngsters or those without

Even a bowl of oatmeal tastes better in the woods, but pancakes hot off the griddle in a high mountain camp may just be the best meal you'll ever eat. Traveling with horses gives a backcountry camper a wider range of gourmet options at mealtimes. (Dale Burk photo)

much hiking experience.

Good maps of the Bitterroot National Forest, available at any Forest Service Ranger Station or the Supervisor's Office in Hamilton, are a tremendous help when trying to find trailheads in the Bitterroot. The profusion of roads, some of them signed and others not, can be more than a bit confusing. Good topographical maps of the trails themselves are also essential to those who want to stay "found."

Hikers and backpackers should carry with them all the essential items they might need, most particularly extra water, and weather gear to handle the worst the season can throw at them. It's no exaggeration to say that in the high country, snow is possible at any time, and even when the temperature is in the 40's or 50's, hypothermia can kill if you get wet. Be prepared!

Ten Essentials

The "ten essentials" is a concept developed decades ago as a basic checklist before venturing out into the woods. It is by no means a complete list of what you should have with you on any given day, but for most day hikes represents a reasonable starting point. Inclusion of an item also presumes some knowledge of its safe and proper use.

1. Map and compass.
2. Flashlight or headlamp.
3. Matches (waterproof) or lighter.
4. Shelter (a sheet of plastic, tarp, or even a couple of garbage bags will serve, in an emergency).
5. Extra food and water.
6. Extra clothing (particularly in the mountains–it cools off dramatically after the sun sets).
7. First aid supplies.
8. Knife.
9. Sunglasses or goggles (winter).
10. Whistle.

As you can see, this is appropriate for a day hike or a hunting pack, but could reasonably be expanded depending on time of year and destination to include more clothing, sunscreen, water purification, and so forth. Reliance on high-tech items such as GPS or a cellular phone is unwise.

Also, always leave word with someone responsible as to where you're going and when you should be expected back.

CLIMBING

The Bitterroot offers a wide range of climbing opportunities. From peaks that can be bagged by any reasonably fit day-hiker, to big granite walls that will challenge the most experienced rock climber, to icy fangs that drip from the canyon walls in winter, no climber needs to walk away unfulfilled.

Rock-climbing and bouldering guides are available at bookstores and sporting-goods stores. Wise climbers will refer to these or consult with local climbers to make sure they don't get in over their heads.

Nearly any canyon offers a challenge to rock climbers, but Kootenai canyon has a well-developed climbing area, and Blodgett canyon offers some difficult but spectacular routes, both bolted and "natural." Blodgett and other canyons also develop some reliable ice climbs in winter. Climbers should always be aware of whether they're climbing on private or public land, and any applicable restrictions.

The most popular "hikeable" peaks in the valley are St. Mary's, at 9,351 feet, and Trapper Peak, the highest in the county, at 10,157 feet. Both trailheads start at over 6,000 feet, so the climbs are strenuous but manageable. Ward Mountain offers a bit more of a workout, with a summit at 9,119 feet, and a trailhead roughly 5,000 feet lower. Take food, water, warm clothing (it's always much cooler and windy on the summits) and keep an eye on the weather.

Mountaineers looking for mixed technical routes will do best in late spring or early summer, when climbing El Capitan, the Como Peaks, or any number of other trailless peaks in the Bitterroot range, offer a mixture of snow, ice, and rock to test your skills (and your judgment). Know your equipment and your limits, and climb with care.

HUNTING

Big-game hunting in Ravalli County is big business. The dedicated hunter will find ample prey: mule deer, whitetail deer, mountain goats, bighorn sheep, black bear, elk, moose, and mountain lions are all fair game, with the proper licenses and tags. Ducks, geese, grouse, pheasant and other upland birds entice wing-shooters in the fall.

Most of the public land in the valley is open to hunting, but check with the appropriate agency first if you have any doubts. Restrictions apply at the Lee Metcalf National Wildlife Refuge, in some State game management areas, and elsewhere.

That still leaves thousands of acres of habitat available for sportsmen.

Sporting Organizations

The Bitterroot not only supports a wide variety of game animals, but also a gaggle of sportsmen's organizations. Trout Unlimited, Ducks Unlimited, Pheasants Forever, the Rocky Mountain Elk Foundation, and the Ravalli County Fish & Wildlife Association all represent the interests of hunters and anglers in the valley. Regardless of your feelings about hunting or fishing, these organizations are responsible for many of the amenities that valley residents find valuable. It is largely through their efforts that water is reserved in Painted Rocks and Como lakes for augmenting low flows in the Bitterroot River, that elk and bighorn sheep now thrive in the valley, and that pheasant are widely distributed throughout the area. They also work hard to preserve water quality and to protect wildlife habitat from encroaching development.

The contributions, both in dollars and volunteer hours, of these organizations to the conservation of natural resources and wildlife, have earned them the respect of those who don't hunt or fish, but who just enjoy the natural environment.

Resident conservation licenses are available at sporting goods shops, where current hunting and fishing regulations should be picked up as well. Special drawings may be necessary for some game species, and regulations vary from year to year. Non-residents should contact the Montana Department of Fish, Wildlife and Parks for hunting regulations and license information.

Numerous outfitters in the valley offer guided hunts and hunting camps for those who appreciate the advantages they offer.

Archery season for big game, and upland bird season opens in early to mid-September, and the general rifle season in late October, running through the Thanksgiving weekend. A spring bear season also attracts many hunters.

SNOW SPORTS

The floor of the lower Bitterroot Valley may be free of snow during winter, but don't be deceived. Four thousand feet higher, the snow conditions are great!

The ski season usually begins some time in November, when the mountains ringing the valley acquire a sufficient covering of snow to attract those who are willing to risk the occasional rock. From then on, it only gets better, until things get too sloppy (for most) in April, although a new generation of hardy snow-shoers keep pushing the season later as they travel the high country.

Downhill skiers and snowboarders are generally drawn to Lost Trail Powder Mountain, a developed ski resort at Lost Trail Pass on Highway 93, on the Idaho border. Lost Trail Powder Mountain's two existing lifts offer access to ski runs from beginner to expert, with 18 runs and 1,200 feet of vertical relief. The mountain receives consistent snow, averaging roughly 300 inches total per year, with an average base of 80 inches. Most of the mountain is groomed, but the steeper runs are left for the powder hounds.

The area's reputation is that of an affordable destination that trades-off its less-than-deluxe accommodations for a very reasonably priced lift ticket accessing exciting runs with consistent snow.

At the time of this writing, Lost Trail Powder Mountain is working on an expansion that will add substantially to their total area, spreading out the skiers over another mountainside and providing plenty of elbow room. Two new lifts will access 222 acres of new terrain, largely intermediate to advanced. A new lodge and warming cabin will serve the expansion, which will more than double the area's capacity.

Cross-country skiers gravitate to nearby Chief Joseph Pass, where the Bitterroot Cross Country Ski Club maintains more than 24 kilometers of groomed ski trails for four months every year, beginning in early December. The terrain is fairly gentle and the snow conditions consistently inviting, adding up to a great outdoor winter activity. Located astride the Continental Divide on Montana Highway 43, the Chief Joseph Pass trails also offer marked but un-groomed trails leading up Anderson Mountain and elsewhere.

For the adventurous, the Wisdom Ranger District of the U.S. Forest Service has several remote cabins available for rent during the winter months, some accessible by ski only, others to snowmobilers as well.

Lolo Pass, atop the Montana/Idaho border on U.S. 12, west of Lolo, also offers excellent cross-country skiing. Be sure to pick up your Idaho Park & Ski sticker for your car before heading up.

Roads and trails at higher elevations throughout the valley provide winter sports access in some years, but snow cover can be highly unpredictable from year to year, so checking on conditions in advance is advisable.

For those to whom winter means an opportunity to leave nearly everyone else

behind, the backcountry skiing opportunities in the Bitterroot are unrivaled. Skiing along the crest of the Sapphire range is possible, and hardy skiers every year pioneer other destinations in the Bitterroot's abundant backcountry. Skiers are well-advised to let someone know where they'll be, when to expect them back, and to carry with them everything they would need for safe travel and several nights out in extreme cold conditions.

The increasing popularity of snowshoeing also draws winter recreationists into the Bitterroot's canyons and mountains. Once again, the list of destinations is limited only by one's imagination and good judgment – a winter night spent unexpectedly outdoors is no picnic. Be ready, and leave word.

Finally, snowmobilers are finding ever more places to take their machines as the technology evolves. Snowmobiles are more capable and more reliable than ever, and organized rides are a frequent winter event in the Bitterroot. Check with the Forest Service or at any of the businesses that rent, sell or service snowmobiles for a map indicating areas where snow machines are permitted.

BOATING AND RAFTING

What happens to all that snow when spring and summer come? It passes under every boat in the Bitterroot on its way to the Pacific.

The Bitterroot river rewards those who float its waters with outstanding scenery, terrific fishing, and opportunities to see a variety of wildlife along its banks. The price of that is portaging around log jams or fallen trees, which the river can sweep you toward with surprising speed at high water, and annoying gravel bars and other hazards at low water. It can also lead to the occasional tragic situation, when someone fails to take the river seriously.

That doesn't deter thousands of people every year who take to the river in rafts, drift boats, kayaks, canoes, and inner tubes every year. The boating season now stretches from the first sunny days in March, through the last bitter afternoons in October, but the heyday lasts from the end of spring runoff season, usually some time in June, through the first frosty days of September.

Access to the river is provided at convenient intervals along its entire length. Nearly every bridge provides a parking area nearby, whether formal or informal, and the Montana Dept. of Fish, Wildlife & Parks also provides formal access at several points. Recreationists are welcome up to the normal high-water mark of the river, but beyond that, please respect private property.

The river is rarely disturbed by the passage of motorized watercraft. Current regulations permit the use of motorized craft from the Florence Bridge downstream to the confluence with the Clark Fork River only during high water, from May 1 through June 30. Craft of under 15 h.p. may also be used from October through January, (an unusual time to go putting up the river).

Boaters, swimmers and jet-skiers also ply the waters of Lake Como, tucked away below El Capitan and the Como Peaks, between Hamilton and Darby. It's

er sports aren't limited to just downhill skiing, but that's a good place to start. Trail Powder Mountain's expansion will make an even greater variety of terrain lable to skiers and snowboarders of all skill levels.

Horseback riding has alw *meant more than mere* *transportation in the Bitte* *Valley. Here, an unknown* *young woman with a* *magnificent mount* *demonstrates a "don't-try* *this-at-home" technique.* *(BRVHS Photo)*

difficult to imagine a more magnificent setting, and people flock to Como for fishing, water skiing, picnicking and any other reason they can think of, just to bask in the scenery and the wildlife. Loons, osprey and eagles may join deer, elk and moose on any given day. By late summer, the mud flats may begin to emerge as the lake is drawn down for irrigation, but by then water anywhere in the valley is a precious commodity and people are grateful to find it in any quantity.

The only other substantial lake in the Bitterroot is Painted Rocks Reservoir, hidden away in what feels like a remote corner of the world, miles up the West Fork of the Bitterroot River. Painted Rocks Reservoir, impounded behind the West Fork Dam, is also seriously drawn down by summer's end, but until that time offers boating opportunities and scenic camping.

The East and West Forks of the Bitterroot may be floated by experienced boaters in most seasons, but it's best to inquire locally first.

HORSEBACK RIDING

Horseback riding isn't just a recreational activity in the Bitterroot. Horses remain an indispensable tool for ranchers and for backcountry outfitters. That isn't to say, though, that they aren't also a popular form of diversion – they are.

Many of the trailheads in the valley offer horse ramps for loading and

The Old-Timer's Rodeo is a sanctioned event that draws experienced competitors to the Ravalli County Fairgrounds arena every year.

unloading stock. Trail riding in the wilderness can be tricky, and inexperienced riders should go with a guide, or with one of the organized rides offered by the Bitterroot Backcountry Horsemen, or other riding organizations.

The Selway-Bitterroot Wilderness is a perfect place to explore with pack stock. The ability to travel farther and carry more gear makes this huge expanse of wilderness far more accessible. Horsemen should check with the Forest Service for current regulations on weed-seed-free feed, party size, and other considerations, and be prepared to deal with trails in less-than-optimum condition. Many trails are recommended for experienced riders only.

Forest Service roads throughout both the Sapphire and Bitterroot ranges also provide excellent opportunities for peaceful riding.

BICYCLING/MOUNTAIN BIKING

Bicyclists find whatever they want in the Bitterroot Valley. Road bikes regularly cruise on the relatively flat roads of the valley floor, while mountain bikers burn their quads up on the roads and trails that lead into the mountains.

For touring bikes, Highway 93 carries a heavy traffic load, but offers ample shoulders that make it somewhat less scary. The Eastside Highway, once a narrow, potholed disaster for cyclists, is being rebuilt with somewhat more accommodating

If no existing sport suits your fancy, take a look around. New sports are being invented almost daily, such as this motorcycle trials event.

shoulders, is extremely scenic and has less traffic. The East and West Fork roads, and side roads such as Sleeping Child, Skalkaho and many roads on the East side of the valley offer terrific touring.

For mountain bikes, just consult your Forest Service map and go. Most of the dirt roads in the valley will provide a scenic workout, and many will lead you to a single-track opportunity. Check with the District Ranger's office first – some trails lead into wilderness, and mountain biking is forbidden. Others welcome bikers–the trail around Lake Como is open, and the trail to Fred Burr Reservoir is a beautiful ride. Be aware that horses may shy from a mounted bicyclist – be courteous and dismount, keeping in plain view on the downhill side of the stock, to avoid problems.

The Bitterroot National Forest publishes handouts on mountain biking opportunities, and local bookstores and sporting goods stores may also carry a mountain biking guide book for the area.

GOLF

Deer are a common hazard at the Whitetail Golf Course adjacent to the Lee Metcalf National Wildlife Refuge, where nine holes are available to links-lovers. In Hamilton, the Hamilton Golf Club offers 18 challenging holes in one of the most beautiful settings anywhere. The Stock Farm is developing a private, 18-hole course, but public access isn't necessarily in the plans at this time.

A driving range along Highway 93 near Corvallis serves those who just want to get out and hit a bucket of balls into the wind.

FLYING, GLIDING AND PARACHUTING

Airports in both Hamilton and Stevensville provide opportunities for scenic flights. Check the phone book for local operators. Flying among the mountains of the Selway-Bitterroot wilderness is an experience never to be forgotten, and backcountry airstrips that were "grandfathered" into the wilderness still serve as a supply line for hikers and floaters on the Selway.

For the more adventurous, parachuting is available in Stevensville, where a short ground school prepares you for a tandem jump, lashed to a jumpmaster, with 30 seconds of free-fall before he or she pulls the ripcord. It won't be the scenery that you remember.

Hamilton is currently home to a glider club that offers rides on an occasional basis. Inquire at the airport for current information.

For those who think smaller, a local remote-control aircraft club also offers a developed "airfield" for hobbyists.

SWIMMING

It's a long way between public pools in the Bitterroot, but at least you're never far from the river or a ditch where you can cool off. Both Hamilton and Stevensville offer public pools in the summer. In other months, you may prefer the warm waters of Lolo Hot Springs, on U.S. 12 west of Lolo, or Lost Trail Hot Springs, at the foot of Lost Trail Pass on Highway 93 south of Darby.

SCENIC DRIVING

The Bitterroot is a place of tremendous beauty, and the best way to enjoy it is to get out in it. For some, though, that's not possible, whether due to physical handicaps or just a shortage of time. The solution: take a scenic drive.

Easily the best place for that is the Eastside Highway, between Florence and Hamilton. This alternate to Highway 93 carries much less traffic (and at a slower pace), offering a chance to enjoy the view. From the middle of the valley, one gets a much broader perspective of the massive Bitterroot range, while enjoying the pastoral foreground of irrigated fields and the protected habitat of the Lee Metcalf National Wildlife Refuge.

From Hamilton, try the Skalkaho Highway. This scenic road (officially designated Montana Highway 38) is paved for 15 miles, then becomes a gravel road suitable for passenger cars, but with caution. Built in the 1920's to provide more direct automobile access to Butte, it is an engineering marvel, but its steep drop-offs and sharp curves are not for the faint-hearted driver.

About 22 miles up, the road passes directly by the beautiful Skalkaho Falls, before crossing the Sapphire Range at Skalkaho Pass, then drops down into the headwaters of Rock Creek, and finally down into the Flint Creek Valley near the community of Philipsburg.

Along the way, about 11 miles from Hamilton, it passes the Centennial Grove, a wheelchair-accessible nature trail with a self-guided tour that identifies the trees, shrubs and plants native to the area.

The Skalkaho Highway is closed in winter months due to snow, and may not be open until some time in June; check with the highway department before attempting to travel it. The highway also develops severe potholes and washboard surfaces, and is narrow, winding, and dusty. It rewards the traveler, though, with beautiful mountain vistas, roaring waterfalls, and tranquil streams.

The East Fork Road will take you past observation points where bands of bighorn sheep frequent the hillsides, to fishing and camping access on the sparkling waters of the East Fork. With a good vehicle, you can take the road up to McCart lookout, an abandoned fire lookout that is available during part of the year for rent, as is the former East Fork Ranger Station. Inquire with the Sula Ranger District.

The West Fork Road also offers some outstanding scenery as it parallels the West Fork of the Bitterroot River. It offers possibilities of connecting with Shoup, Idaho, on the Salmon River, or Elk City, Idaho, passing through the Magruder Corridor and crossing the Wild & Scenic Selway River.

CABIN RENTALS

The Bitterroot National Forest offers several unique recreation opportunities. A number of cabins – and one abandoned lookout tower – are maintained for rental. These include the East Fork Guard Station, relatively deluxe in that you can drive to it most of the year and it has electricity, and the contrasting McCart Lookout Tower, which involves a mile-and-a-half hike, and where no water or electricity is available.

Stock Farm golf course and clubhouse beckon to those who take their links time ᴐusly.

The remote Twogood cabin and the Woods cabin on Lake Como also offer vastly differing opportunities, the former six miles up a trail near Sula, and offering the bare necessities for six friendly people, the latter with drive-up convenience and three bedrooms to accommodate up to 15 at a popular recreation site. Contact the Bitterroot National Forest for further information on these, and other, recreation opportunities.

Starting in late September, the summits of the Bitterroots are decorated in gold, as the subalpine larch turn color. From the top of Downing Mountain, Hamilton is framed by this unique species, found only in the northern Rockies. (R. Lawrence photo)

PART FOUR: CULTURAL OPPORTUNITIES

Anyone who thinks the Bitterroot is lacking in cultural opportunities isn't paying attention. Granted, you won't find a resident symphony orchestra or even "name-brand" touring companies in the valley, but the overall availability of the arts is quite satisfying. You may have to look beyond the casino-lined main streets to find it, but the valley's communities have forged a strong artistic presence.

The valley is still a do-it-yourself kind of place. Most of the arts events that take place here are hands-on, grassroots efforts put together by people who share an interest. The Bitterroot is a place for participants, not just observers.

THEATRE

The spirit of community theatre thrives in the valley. Both Stevensville and Hamilton support theatre companies that produce numerous shows every year.

In Hamilton, the Hamilton Players have renovated a historic old schoolhouse into the comfortable Hamilton Playhouse, a mile west of town on Ricketts Road. Here, in their 196-seat theatre, they have produced musicals, comedies, and dramas, ranging from intricate and demanding musicals to a locally-produced live radio broadcast.

The Hamilton Players typically produce four plays of their own in a year, and encourage touring companies and others to make use of their facility, which has seen dance recitals, classical music concerts, and even weddings.

In Stevensville, the Chantilly Theatre produces a full season of shows every year in their intimate, 99-seat house, remodeled from the former Rio movie house. Typical fare ranges from musicals to works by local playwrights, and their stage is available for other events as well.

Theatre in Darby is on a more ad hoc basis, but the Community Arts and Recreation Program (C.A.R.P.) sponsors events of all kinds.

On a regular basis, the Bozeman-based "Shakespeare in the Parks" touring company visits Hamilton on a summer evening, presenting works of the Bard or his contemporaries, outdoors, at the tops of their lungs and at a frantic pace.

MUSIC

The opportunities to hear live music in the valley are abundant and extend well beyond the Friday and Saturday-night bar and restaurant scene, although that's usually an option, too.

•The Bitterroot Concert Association produces a number of classical music concerts throughout the year, frequently including a summer concert at the Daly Mansion.

•The Bitterroot Community Band makes music every summer (and as needed throughout the year), showing up at many community events and staging concerts at various locations.

•"Tuesday at Twelve" is a series of free summer concerts every Tuesday noon in Hamilton's Legion Park during the summer, featuring a variety of musical styles, food vendors, picnic blankets spread out and a relaxed crowd.

•The Bitterroot Bluegrass Festival is a July event featuring both the best of the local players and a handful of performers on the summer festival circuit.

The opportunities to make music and to hear music informally are too numerous to keep track of, but if you are a skilled musician in the Bitterroot, you'll have an opportunity to perform.

VISUAL ARTS

"Art in the Park," a late-July art show in Hamilton's Legion Park is the high point of the Arts Guild's annual efforts, although by no means its only effort. This alliance of painters and craftspeople also presents its work to the public in a winter show, and the work of these artists appears everywhere in the valley–galleries, banks and other public buildings, restaurants, and gift shops.

Several galleries dot the valley, and other "lifestyle" shops have also sprung up, featuring both fine art and beautiful crafts by local residents.

MUSEUMS

The Ravalli County Museum is a medium-sized treasure. Occupying the former County Courthouse building (which voters elected to save rather than raze when the current courthouse was built in the 1970's), the museum houses both numerous displays open to the public, and an extensive collection of books, newspapers and original documents for research purposes. Displays depict aspects of Bitterroot history and culture, ranging from the Tick Fever room to a display dedicated to fly-fishing.

The Ravalli County Museum sponsors several notable events on both a weekly and an annual basis. Bitterroot Day is typically a Sunday in June, when the museum is decorated with bitterroot flowers from the garden of Henry Grant who, during his lifetime, devoted himself to everything connected to the flower, and the valley bearing its name. October brings MacIntosh Apple Days, a celebration with craft vendors, entertainment, and apples, apples, apples. A cauldron of savory apple butter, pies galore, caramel apples, and other apple-related goodies grace the grounds of the museum in a celebration of the Bitterroot's orchard heritage. Finally, they sponsor the Sunday Series, a weekly offering of lectures, performances, or special exhibits nearly every Sunday at 2 p.m.

The Daly Mansion offers programs and opportunities throughout the year, ranging from doll shows to spectacular Christmas decorations and crafts.

A wide variety of specialized shows and exhibitions take place throughout the year, including spinning, weaving and other fiber arts, dance recitals performed by students of various schools, car shows and other events.

Victor, Stevensville and Darby also support small museums with photos,

...1 given the choice, voters in the 1970's elected to preserve the original county ...house, designed by the noted architect A. J. Gibson and built in 1899. It now ...es the popular Ravalli County Museum.

artifacts, and knowledgeable volunteers to bring their community's story to life.

FESTIVALS

Every community in the valley seems to want to commemorate itself with a summer festival (or two), and a person could become exhausted visiting them all. Each has a slightly different flavor, and even this may vary from year to year, but that simply adds to their unique character. The dates vary every year, but watch out from early June until late August for these and other celebrations:

•The Corvallis Memorial Day Parade usually kicks off summer with a parade sponsored by the town's American Legion post and auxiliary. Watch the entries proceed down the short Main Street, turn around, and march right back!

•The Darby Strawberry Festival is a town-wide, old-fashioned ice cream social, usually with live music, and staggering amounts of strawberry shortcake.

•Darby Fun Days fills the town for events and mingling.

•Western Days celebrates Stevensville's heritage as Montana's first community.

•Hamilton's Summerfest usually closes off Main Street for music, food, contests and other events, sometimes including a Microbrew festival.

•The Victor Civic Club sponsors Chief Victor Days, which fills the Victor park with music, arts and crafts, and contests for the kids, usually in mid-July.

An unknown group of young men from the "Music Man" era get together to make music, a summer-time tradition carried on now by the Bitterroot Community Band. Band instrument companies would ship an assortment of instruments, uniforms, sheet music and instructions as a package deal, and it was the rare community that didn't sport at least one brass ensemble. (BRVHS Photo)

•The Stevensville Creamery Picnic, held the first weekend in August, is the small-town event of the year. A parade, arts and crafts booths, food booths, contests, music, and other events spread out over a weekend that leaves the entire community grinning. The event commemorates the disastrous fire in 1911 that destroyed John Howe's creamery. The town rallied to help him build a new one, double the size of the ruined facility, and it was completed in six weeks. Delighted, Howe threw a huge, community picnic celebration when it opened in August, and the event became an annual institution.

•The Ravalli County Fair deserves a category of its own. This late-August, early-September event brings the entire valley together like no other occasion. A family-oriented affair, with no alcohol permitted on the fairgrounds, the Ravalli County Fair simply can't be missed. It features a rodeo, midway rides and games, food booths too numerous to contemplate, exhibitions of livestock, autos, artwork, agricultural products, commercial exhibits, 4-H projects, canned items, baked goods, needle arts, and performers, and a miles-long Fair Parade down Hamilton's Main Street.

Horse racing was long a part of the Ravalli County Fair, but economics and other considerations put an end to it, although periodic efforts to resurrect the race

Darby enters the next phase of its evolution from logging town to recreation capital of the south valley. With a spruced-up Main Street and a colorful past, the town is ready to try on a new identity.

meet have met with mixed success. Marcus Daly would have been disappointed.

•The Hamilton Farmer's Market is a bustling sight on a Saturday morning in the summer. Held at the Ravalli County Museum, it features local produce and crafts from 9-12, typically from June through August. Vendors and shoppers alike are frequently entertained by musical offerings. Victor also currently offers a market on Sunday mornings from 8-12.

The valley offers far more than this sampling of community events. Special interests sponsor events nearly every week, with horse events dominating the fairgrounds in summer, art & craft events of all kinds, motor sports, athletic events and other gatherings all seemingly happening the same weekend you planned to stay home quietly . . .

Bitterroot Good Nations Powwow, held at the Daly Mansion in the heat of July,
traditional Indian dancers a chance to strut. Some dances are open to all
ers, others are restricted. Organizers are glad to explain the protocol to
omers.

Old meets new: hitching posts are a thing of the past, but drive-up windows don't discriminate between carriages, horseless and otherwise.

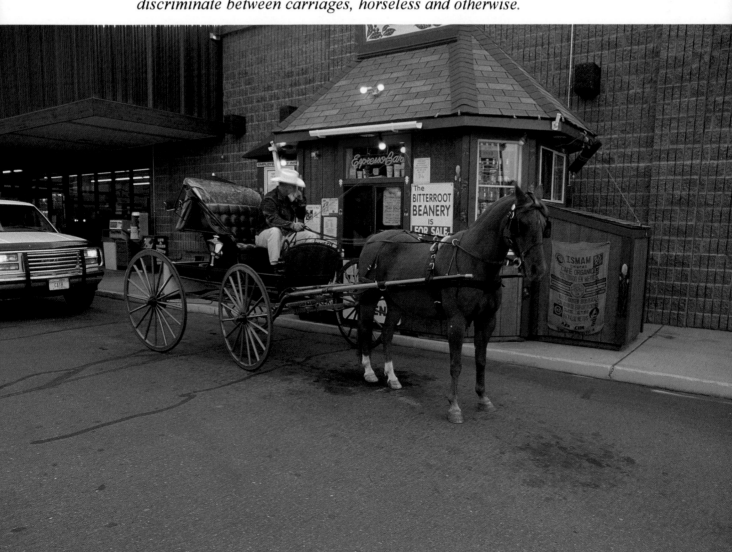

PART FIVE: THE BITTERROOT TODAY

Ravalli County has, for the last decade, been one of the fastest-growing counties in Montana. For that reason, any statistical information given here is automatically suspect, but useful nonetheless as a guide.

AREA: Ravalli County encompasses 2,400 square miles, roughly 25 miles east-to-west, and 96 miles north to south. Okay, call it an even 100 miles, more or less. Let's not worry about the county line. Within Ravalli County, approximately 74% of the land is in public hands (federal and state ownership), with 26% privately held.

ELEVATION: Elevation ranges from approximately 3,200 feet at the mouth of the Bitterroot River, to 10,157 feet atop Trapper Peak, southwest of Darby. Stevensville's elevation is 3,370, Hamilton's is 3,572, and Darby sits 3,887 feet above sea level.

POPULATION: Estimates for the year 2000 yield about 37,000 people in Ravalli County. The figure for Hamilton is 4,200–5,000 (varying estimates), Stevensville about 2,000, and Darby between 800-900. Other unincorporated communities are harder to define, but Lolo is estimated at 2,400, Florence 1,200, Victor 350, Corvallis 400, Pinesdale 500, Grantsdale 650.

ECONOMIC PORTRAIT

Ask anyone – wages are low in the Bitterroot. The cost of living is somewhat lower than average as well, but not proportional to the wage gap. You pay an economic penalty for living here, there's little doubt, with per capita wages running as low as 69% of the national average, and that figure has been slipping for twenty years. The consistent growth in population, however, indicates that the non-economic amenities the valley affords continue to more than make up the difference.

The economic base of the valley has shifted dramatically over the last century, as logging and agriculture, the base on which it was built, have declined, and many of the related jobs and services have moved or disappeared. In their place, a number of industries have remained or emerged to give the Bitterroot a unique identity. For instance, between Marcus Daly Memorial Hospital (currently the largest private employer in the valley), the Rocky Mountain Lab, and Corixa Corporation (formerly Ribi Immunochem Research, Inc.), the Bitterroot has a disproportionate number of well-educated professionals from the health sciences field.

The valley's reputation as a retirement area may be somewhat overstated, but the health and elder-care facilities (nursing homes, assisted living centers), and "retirement living" facilities also factor into the strong health and services sector of the economy.

rosty morning turns an irrigation line into sparkling sculpture.

Ribi Immunochem

Ribi Immunochem (now Corixa) was started in 1981 by Edgar Ribi, a scientist, and others who believed they could discover and produce valuable drugs, building on research begun at the Rocky Mountain Lab. The company began developing its biopharmaceuticals and immunostimulants at a small facility in Hamilton, quickly moving to a modern research and production plant they built north of town on Old Corvallis Road.

Early on, Ribi's researchers produced drugs that showed promise in reducing tumors in animals by stimulating their own immune response, and adjuvants, materials that enhanced the performance of other drugs when administered together.

The company suffered a setback when founder Edgar Ribi died in the crash of his small plane near Lookout Pass in 1987, but the research staff and management were in place to carry on the company's mission.

Although the company expanded in the early 90's to increase production of its flagship pharmaceuticals, it never turned a profit. Investors, though, believed that its long-term potential remained very good, based on the direction of research and the money that could be realized when Ribi's products were cleared for human use.

The effect of Corixa's purchase of the company remains to be seen, but most expect the firm to remain a significant contributor to Hamilton's economy.

First cutting of hay, or second? Judging from the lack of snow on the mountains, probably the latter. Hay remains an important crop for Bitterroot ag producers, and a healthy second cutting in the summer can make a critical difference when a hard winter hangs on late.

The log-home industry is the most visible manufacturing component of the valley's economy, shipping their products to local buyers as well as overseas customers.

Even casual observers are impressed by the number of log home manufacturers here. Many are highly visible along U.S. 93, but others are scattered out of sight. They continue to flourish long after the factors that attracted them here in the first place have disappeared.

Those factors included ready access to a huge amount of standing dead lodgepole pine, fire-killed by the Sleeping Child and Saddle Mountain burns of the early 60's. This timber was ideally suited to log home building, and once one or two companies pioneered the field, others "piled-on" in typical Bitterroot fashion. It has been a growth market for more than two decades.

Manufacturers are split between those who design "custom" homes and those that offer "packaged" blueprints, with further refinements between those that notch and fit each log individually, versus those that mill the logs to uniform dimensions for ease of assembly.

Few rely on Bitterroot logs any more, although some salvage sales do occur following fires. More commonly they obtain logs from throughout the Northwest or Canada, and they now market not only throughout North America, but to markets in Europe and Asia as well.

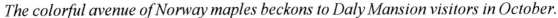

The colorful avenue of Norway maples beckons to Daly Mansion visitors in October.

Tourism constitutes another critical piece of the valley's economic puzzle. Employment related to this industry extends beyond the obvious – hotels and restaurants – to include fishing and hunting guides, outfitters, golf pros, and even real estate agents.

Real estate speculation has been a valley hallmark since the Apple Boom days. The valley experienced a real estate boom in the 1970's, and again in the late 80's and early 90's. Growth remains strong, particularly in the north end of the valley, within commuting range of Missoula.

Agriculture is not the dominant economic player it once was, although it remains highly visible. Cattle prices have not justified strong investment recently, although the ratio of cattle to people in the valley remains fairly close. Barley, wheat and oats are still grown locally, and producers put up tons of hay, typically in two cuttings, every summer.

Finally, the government sector is strong, although the figures may be skewed depending on how one views employees of the Rocky Mountain Lab, a federal government (National Institute of Health) facility.

Here's a breakdown by sector, based on 1997 figures from the U.S. Dept. of Commerce:

Per Capita Income in Ravalli County: $16,584 (roughly 70% of the national average).

Income by Industry	Percent of Total Income
Agriculture	1%
Construction	12
Finance, Insurance, Real Estate	7
Government	17
Manufacturing	13
Mining	1
Services	24 (Health Services = approx. 12%)
Transportation	6
Retail Trade	14
Wholesale Trade	5

The valley is served by three banks with branches in nearly every community, several Savings & Loans, and two credit unions.

TRANSPORTATION

U.S. Highway 93 is the dominant artery of transportation within the Bitterroot Valley. It is paralleled between Florence and Hamilton by the Eastside Highway, and U.S. Highway 12 intersects it at Lolo. The East Fork Road and the West Fork Road provide all-weather access to those areas of the valley. The nearest Interstate Highway is I-90, which passes along the northern part of the Missoula Valley, 50 miles north of Hamilton.

Montana Rail Link has rail service to Hamilton, with tracks running as far as Darby.

Two paved runways serve air traffic in the valley. The Ravalli County Airport in Hamilton offers a lighted, 4,200-foot runway, with fuel (piston & jet) and mechanics on the field. The Stevensville airport has a 3,800-foot runway, repair service, and piston-engine fuel.

GOVERNMENT: Ravalli County is governed by three county commissioners. The four incorporated communities all have a form of Mayor/Council government. Seven school districts serve the county.

LAND USE & PLANNING

Planning is a sore subject in the Bitterroot, both for those who oppose it in any form, and for those who bemoan the lack of it.

Ravalli County lacks a current Master Plan, and in its absence a hodgepodge of neighborhood zoning efforts have arisen, some more successful than others. Most of the county remains without any form of zoning, though, and this has led to increasing conflicts.

Even before the highway was paved, the Missoula – Hamilton Stage, operated by Jack Centers, offered deluxe transportation over the 50 rough miles linking the two towns. Made from a stretched Pierce-Arrow, it modestly avoided mixing the sexes on the jostling ride. (BRVHS Photo)

On one extreme are those who insist that any planning or zoning document is an infringement of private property rights, that individuals should be free to do with their property as they please. On the other extreme are those who insist that what happens on their neighbor's property affects their own property values, and that their neighbor not be allowed to do anything that degrades their own investment. Finding the middle ground has been the elusive grail for twenty years.

Meanwhile, residential subdivisions and commercial developments are approved by County Commissioners who have few grounds for stopping them, barring demonstrable public hazard.

Those who favor planning can encourage neighborhood zoning, which results in a patchwork of regulations, or they can encourage the use of conservation easements or other legal means of protecting real estate from development.

The moment may have passed, though, at least in some areas. The Highway 93 corridor through the valley may once have been among the most scenic in the nation, offering stunning views of the Bitterroots over a pastoral foreground for miles at a time. As it passes through the communities of the valley, though, it is increasingly crowded by haphazard "strip" development, which spills ever farther out beyond the towns. These strips are characterized by the same stores you might see anywhere in the country, crowding out the locally-owned businesses that provide an area's flavor.

Efforts are under way to ensure that the communities retain some of their historic character, and to keep the highway and its associated development from dominating the valley, but it's a difficult proposition.

A visit by several aircraft to the Ravalli County Fairgrounds was the occasion, but oh, those late-20's fashions! (BRVHS Photo)

CONCLUSION

The Bitterroot Valley has much to offer, but as every generation discovers, nobody seems to be satisfied by everything about it. Long-term residents sometimes resent the influx of newcomers, who bring new opportunities to the valley along with the demands they place on its resources. They, in turn, may be frustrated by the valley's resistance to the inevitability of change.

The happiest residents, though, are those who see what is spectacularly right about the Bitterroot: the river, the mountains, the climate, the accessibility of both cultural and natural resources. They adapt to what can't be changed, and spend what time they can working to improve the rest.

You'll see them often, smiling to themselves on the street, on the trail, or on a ski run – but not talking on a cell phone in their car. When you see them, smile back and nod. It's the universal sign of someone who has made peace with living in a place that's always one step short of Paradise.

BIBLIOGRAPHY

A Traveler's Companion to Montana History, by Carol Van West, Montana Historical Society, 1986.

Bitterroot Trails, Vols. I and II, by Lena Bell, Henry Grant, and Phyllis Twogood, Bitter Root Valley Historical Society, 1982.

Bitter Root Trails III, Bitter Root Valley Historical Society, 1998.

Flathead Indians, by John Fahey, University of Oklahoma Press, 1974.

Flathead & Kootenay by Olga Johnson, Northwest Historical Series, Arthur H. Clark, 1969.

Good Samaritan of the Northwest, by Lucylle Evans, Montana Creative Consultants, 1981.

Handbook of North American Indians, Volume 12: Plateau, Deward E. Walker, Jr., Editor, Smithsonian Institution, 1998.

Lewis & Clark in the Bitterroot, by The Discovery Writers, Stoneydale Press, 1998.

Montana Genesis, by the Stevensville Historical Society, Mountain Press Publishing, 1971.

Names on the Face of Montana, by Roberta Cheney, Mountain Press Publishing, 1983.

Riverside, by Miriam Poe Ryan, Self-published, 1994.

Roadside Geology of Montana, by David Alt & Donald Hyndman, Mountain Press Publishing, 1986.

Roadside History of Montana, by Don Spritzer, Mountain Press Publishing, 1999.

St. Mary's in the Rocky Mountains, by Lucylle Evans, Montana Creative Consultants, 1976.

BITTERROOT VALLEY RESOURCES

Bitterroot National Forest
Supervisor's Office
1801 N. 1st St.
Hamilton MT 59840
406-363-7117

Bitterroot Valley Chamber of Commerce
105 E. Main
Hamilton MT 59840
406-363-2400

Darby Historic Ranger Station
Highway 93
Darby MT 59829
406-821-3913

Lee Metcalf National Wildlife Refuge
P.O. Box 257
Stevensville MT 59870
406-777-5552

Ravalli County Fish & Wildlife Association
Box238
Hamilton MT 59840

Ravalli County Museum
205 Bedford
Hamilton MT 59840
406-363-3338

St. Mary's Mission
P.O. Box 211
Stevensville MT 59870
406-777-5734

Stevensville Historical Museum
517 Main St.
Stevensville MT 59870
406-777-3201

Teller Wildlife Refuge
1292 Chaffin Road
Corvallis MT 59828
406-961-8346

Victor Heritage Museum
Main & Blake
Victor MT 59875
406-642-3997